Walkin' with God Ain't for Wimps

Karen O'Connor

HARVEST HOUSE PUBLISHERS

EUGENE, OREGON

Karen O'Connor: Published in association with the Books & Such Literary Agency, 52 Mission Circle, Suite 122, PMB 170, Santa Rosa, CA 95409-5370, www.booksandsuch. biz.

Cover by Dugan Design Group, Bloomington, Minnesota

Cover illustration by Dugan Design Group

WALKIN' WITH GOD AIN'T FOR WIMPS
Copyright © 2007 by Karen O'Connor
Published by Harvest House Publishers
Eugene, Oregon 97402

Library of Congress cataloging-in-publication data
    O'Connor, Karen, 1938-
    Walkin' with God ain't for wimps / Karen O'Connor.
        p. cm.
    ISBN-13: 978-0-7369-2038-4 (pbk.)
    ISBN-10: 0-7369-2038-2 (pbk.)
    1. Spirituality. 2. Devotional literature. I. Title
    BV4501.3.O326 2007
    242—dc22
                                                                        2007002503

A Note from Karen

I hope you enjoy this selection of original stories as well as the Bible verses and prayers. May they inspire you to walk with God day by day. And may the stories also bring smiles and chuckles of recognition. Walkin' with God ain't for wimps to be sure. It takes courage and commitment. The readings in this book focus on God's love, care, and forgiveness for every one of His children. We're all in this together!

Karen O'Connor

Acknowledgments

The author wishes to thank the following men and women for contributing their ideas, experiences, and story seeds—all of which have been woven into the fabric of this book in a creative way.

Barbara Anson • Betty Blyler • Dale and Dolores Collins • Charles Flowers • Dianne Geisler • Kathleen Gibson • Joann Hawkins • Linda Jewell • Irma Newland • Penny Pfister Newland • June O'Connor • Angela Pisel • Marilyn Prasow • Laura Deaton Russell • Kathy Thomas • Erin Torr • Claudia Russell Ward • Mary Yerkes

Contents

Take Five

Walkin' and Talkin'

1

A Funny Thing Happened on My Way to Pray

Ellie set out her devotional, Bible, journal, and pen. She slipped into her pink chenille bathrobe and matching slippers and padded into the living room. She turned on the lamp over the rocker next to the window overlooking the garden. All set.

Not quite. She forgot her cup of tea sitting on the counter in the kitchen. *I must have my tea. Prayer time simply isn't the same without it,* she reminded herself. But as she passed the fridge, Ellie saw a note she had posted there the night before: Take Ralph's blue suit to the cleaners.

Good thing I wrote that reminder or the suit would have stayed in the closet all week. When it came time to put it on for Iris and John's anniversary dinner and dance, Ralph would have been so disappointed. The soup spatter from last week would still be there.

Ellie went to the closet right away, took out the suit, and put it by the front door.

Now where was I? On my way to pray, that's right.

The tea. She picked up the cup but noticed it had cooled off so she popped it into the microwave for a quick nuke. A moment later it was piping hot again. Ellie dropped in a dollop of honey, and then walked back to the living room. As she sat down, she saw a spider spinning a dainty little web in the corner above the piano. *Drat! I hate to disturb his endeavor, but I simply can't bear spiders sharing my home.*

Ellie grabbed a tissue from her pocket, lifted the poor fellow out of the web, and let him loose in the garden. *I hope he'll find a lovely spot among the flowers to rebuild his home. There are so many pretty places to choose from.*

Back to the living room and her favorite chair. Finally it was time to curl up, talk to God, and make a few notations in her journal. There was so much to thank Him for. Ellie enjoyed creating her own hymn of praise, singing to the Lord with pen and paper, musing about the wonderful things He had done in her life. The gift of her dear husband, Ralph, was on top of Ellie's list. Mindy, her cat, was right up there too. And, of course, her three adult children and all the grandkids.

"I picked up my pen, opened the journal, and was jarred out of my senses with the sound of the phone. Wouldn't you know it? I had forgotten to bring it with me. I was so busy with tea and prayer books and itsy bitsy spider!"

It was Ellie's neighbor Barbara calling. She needed a ride to the hairdresser. With a broken right arm, she couldn't drive for at least six weeks. Ellie agreed to help, of course, but Barbara wanted to leave in 30 minutes.

"Here I was hardly dressed to go out, and I still hadn't started my prayer time." Ellie was frustrated with all the distractions, but then a funny thing happened. The Lord dropped into her mind the verse that says to pray without ceasing.

Perfect timing, she thought. *It's nice when I can settle down in one place and focus on a list of things to write about and read and pray for in a logical and orderly way. But it's also perfectly fine to pray moment-by-moment while I pour a cup of tea, make the bed, take Ralph's suit to the cleaners, and visit with Barbara while we drive to her appointment.*

Ellie thought about how God is everywhere and ever with her, in the mundane and in the mysteries of life. Prayer time is any time and all the time. *My very life can be a prayer. God is pleased with me just the way I am, wherever I am. I love Him, and I know He loves me!*

Reflection

Pray without ceasing (1 Thessalonians 5:17 KJV).

God, it is so easy to become distracted by the cares of the world, the small duties that so easily consume my day and the people who flow in and out of my life. Help me to include all of this in my daily prayers as I walk with You from sunrise to sunset.

2

Now Hear This

"Mom and Dad visit us every summer," Emily shared. "They arrive on Memorial Day weekend and stay through Labor Day. I have loved these extended times together, but as the years pass, things are changing. They just don't hear as well as they used to."

Emily and her husband, Roy, decided to do something about it. They were frustrated with having to repeat themselves. It also bothered them that Emily's parents couldn't hear each other. "What'd you say?" "Speak louder." "Can't get it. Say it again." These became stock phrases around their home.

One day Emily took matters into her own hands. "Mom and Dad," she announced, "today Roy and I are taking you out to buy top-of-the-line hearing aids. It's an early Christmas present to you," she said smiling. "And one to us!" she added under her breath.

The four made the rounds, and then settled on a store that sold exactly what they were hoping for. The older couple was fitted for the aids, and Roy paid for them. Afterward they went to lunch to celebrate. Emily was relieved to know that now even in a noisy restaurant she and her mother could converse without questioning looks and misunderstandings.

They arrived at Sheldon's Deli for their favorite corned beef sandwiches on rye with a dill pickle on the side. Her mom and dad slid into one side of the booth, and Emily and Roy took the other side.

Margie, the server, approached their table and passed out menus. They placed their order, and Margie went off to fill it.

Emily leaned over to her mother and asked how the hearing aids felt: "Do you notice a difference?"

Her mother winked. "Oh yes. They're working so well, I can almost hear your thoughts!"

Emily laughed. She appreciated her mother's sense of humor. She was taking this symptom of old age in stride. Emily hoped she'd be as gracious when her time came.

The server arrived and set out the sandwiches. Then she passed out the drinks: a strawberry malt for Emily, lemonade for Emily's mom, and iced tea for the men.

Emily noticed her mother looking around for something. "What do you need, Mom?"

"Please pass the salt."

Emily smiled and pushed her malt across the table. She was happy to share a sip with her mother.

"Salt, dear. S-A-L-T," her mother repeated in a loud voice.

"Sorry, Mom. What? Say that again."

Her mother mimicked pouring salt. "SALT," she called, cupping her mouth with her hands. Then she pointed to her hearing aid. "No worries, Emily. I know just what you need, and I now know where to get it!"

Emily wanted to slide under the table. "You got me there, Mom," she admitted as she sipped her malt—and passed the salt.

Reflection

Bring me any case too hard for you,
and I will hear it (Deuteronomy 1:17).

Lord, aren't I the know-it-all sometimes? Impatient with the shortcomings of others—even my own parents—until I see how imperfect I am. Thanks for listening, dear God, and for speaking so clearly that I get it with or without hearing aids.

3

Hey, God,
Got a Minute?

Did you ever tug on your mother's pant leg or skirt? You wanted and needed her attention *right now* but she was doing chores. Or maybe it was your father you wanted to speak with. But he was too busy for you to interrupt. It's not like that with God. He's *never* preoccupied with other people or other matters when it comes to *you*. He's all ears! He wants to hear from you about anything and everything. No tugging necessary to get Him to turn your way.

I found that out years ago when I was heartsick over a close friend dropping me for a reason I still don't understand. I didn't feel comfortable calling my mother or sisters with this. And it was not the kind of thing I'd tell a neighbor or a stranger. I bore the hurt alone... until I realized God was not only available, but was actually eager to listen and counsel me.

"Hey, God, got a minute?" I cried out.

He impressed upon my heart that He not only had a minute, He had all the time I needed. That realization alone was enough to ease my hurting heart. I poured out the pain and asked for understanding and empathy for myself and for the other person. I emptied my mind and opened my soul. I told God everything—even the bitter feelings I harbored, the anger I felt against this woman, and the shameful

17

thoughts I carried about her. By the time I took a breath, I felt so much better. I was a child again, sitting at my Father's feet where I belonged, resting in His wisdom and love. It was then I was able to once again speak only what is helpful and beneficial to others. After unburdening myself with God, I could accept, live, and even offer His grace.

Funny how it can take decades to get this truth. If you're facing a predicament that feels huge, go to God first and ask Him to hear you out. He'll do it. There's nothing you can't share with Him. He knows everything already. The next time you're feeling hurt, helpless, alone, or afraid, don't wait. Call out, "Hey, God, got a minute?" He'll be there.

Reflection

Do not let any unwholesome talk come out of your mouths, but only what is helpful for building others up according to their needs, that it may benefit those who listen (Ephesians 4:29).

Lord, too often I speak and think words and thoughts that dishonor You and others because I'm trying to fix things in my own power. But when I call on You, You hear and answer, and I am restored by Your grace so I can keep on walkin' and talkin' with You.

4

Nothin' to Stew About

Rose could hardly wait to board the train from Kalamazoo, Michigan, to Chicago, Illinois. She was one of ten men and women from her church invited to participate in an outreach to inner-city families. Her duties included cooking, facilitating a Bible study for the women and men, playing with the children, and caring for the elderly.

Rose was no youngster herself, but she was still strong and ablebodied. She had plenty of life experience to share with these weary families who had so little—some not even enough food to keep body and soul together.

The first evening there, Rose volunteered to lead worship and to set up a room for the Bible study. She was comfortable in front of a group, and she was especially excited about bringing the Word of God to these people. Just as she was about to test the microphone and put the last few chairs in place, one of the ministers from the host church came up to her. "I heard you make a mean beef stew," he said. "I'd like you to take over in the kitchen. Things are pretty rowdy back there. One of the deacons mentioned you can pull a meal together in minutes—even for a big crowd."

"But I'm in the middle of…" She pointed to the room set-up.

"No problem," he said. "We'll get one of the men to finish the job." The minister walked away.

Rose was insulted. *Just like a man,* she thought. *Stick the women in the kitchen and put the men up front.* "God, this is not fair!" she moaned. She had her heart set on sharing Jesus with the crowd, not being stuck in front of an old stove in an ancient kitchen. But she didn't have a choice. The minister had practically ordered her to cook the meal. She made her way to the kitchen. She peeled the carrots, chopped up the stew meat, cut the potatoes—grumbling with every stroke of the knife.

Then an amazing thing happened. Mothers and fathers and toddlers and teens and boys and girls in-between were walking hand-in-hand in front of the kitchen window on their way to the meeting hall. The setting sun glistened in the background and soft music began to play from the overhead speaker. "Jesus loves me, this I know..."

Rose stopped for a moment, looked out, and listened. *What a scene! People walking and talking together on their way to hear the Word of God. What we came for is already taking place.*

The team was serving these people by their very presence. The families were excited judging from the lilt in their voices and the quickness of their steps.

"To think that just a few moments ago I was caught up in my own delusion of what my mission should be," Rose mused. "I wanted to serve God and these people in *my* way, not God's."

Rose turned back to the stove and the huge cauldron of stew on the back burner. She pulled it to the front, added more carrots, potatoes, and a can of corn. *Imagine this! I get to be the "chef for the day" in the Lord's kitchen. What an honor!*

Rose dipped a ladle into the pot and brought up enough stew to taste. Hands down, it was the best stew she'd ever made!

Reflection

The kingdom of God is not a matter of eating
and drinking, but of righteousness, peace and joy in
the Holy Spirit (Romans 14:17).

*Lord, thank You for showing me that my agenda has more
to do with pleasing and serving myself than doing what will
bless and encourage Your people. Help me mend my selfish
ways and lean on You for direction.*

5

My Way or
the Highway

Fiona and Frank quibbled one morning about how to load the dish-washer. Frank liked to do things according to the manual: glasses and small items on the top rack, plates and pots on the bottom, sil-verware up, not down. Fiona couldn't believe her husband could be so…so self-righteous about such a silly thing. She would *never* dream of making a big deal out of something that could so easily divide them. Life is too short for such nonsense. That was her motto.

She put her arms around her husband. "Honey, does it really matter how the dishes are stacked as long as they get clean?"

He frowned, but then smiled. She could tell her gentle communi-cation had touched him.

The following evening they were on their way to the airport to pick up Fiona's sister and brother-in-law, who were coming in for the weekend. Frank drove, but Fiona couldn't for the life of her figure out why he was taking such a circuitous route, especially when they had cut the timing so close. The plane would be landing in 30 minutes, and they were still 20 minutes away. Her palms grew moist, and she felt a headache coming on.

"It's not too late to backtrack a bit," Fiona said. "We can take the route I always go. I can show you. It's much shorter and there's less traffic. Turn right at the…"

Frank glared. "And with all the time we'll save, we can stop back home and reload the dishwasher the *right* way."

Fiona was crushed. She'd only wanted to be helpful. But then she saw his point. What difference did it make which route they took as long as they got to the airport on time?

Fiona apologized to Frank and thanked him for driving.

Reflection

May the Lord of peace himself give you peace at
all times and in every way (2 Thessalonians 3:16).

Lord, thank You for cutting me off at the pass when I'm about to offer unasked for advice or unwanted commentary. May I leash my tongue and turn to You instead for wisdom and guidance.

6

All Talked Out

My husband, Charles, and I felt led to move closer to one of our daughters and her family in California. We prayed and talked about it, and then prayed some more. Each time we looked at the prospect of living just a short car ride from three of our grandchildren, the more excited we got. We knew the Lord was in this process. We felt His encouragement, and we watched for indications that would confirm our decisions along the way. We stepped out in faith and purchased a small, new home in an over-55 development near our daughter. As my husband said, "We more than qualify."

With expectations high, we put our current home—a condo with a bay view—on the market in January. Here we are nearly seven months later, and we've not received even one offer—just lots of compliments on the view and on our decorating. But we can't take those to the bank. The real estate market in our community, as elsewhere, is flat.

The escrow on our new house closed a month ago, and the new place is ready for us to move into. At the moment it doesn't feel like the sweet deal we envisioned: to sell one at a good price, buy the other for a lower price, and be able to live comfortably as we grow older. Suddenly we own *two* homes, and we have *two* mortgages. That ain't fun!

I am reminding God that *He* gave us these marching orders and

He gave us the high sign every step of the way, so why does it seem as if He has stopped paying attention? Why hasn't He given us the clear signal to go so we can do what He said to do?

I'm all talked out. I have no idea how God will work this out, but I do know that He's God and I'm not. I need to rest in Him and wait for His surprise, whatever and whenever that might be. I'll keep walkin' with Him, but He sure does take His time. In the long run, His plan will work for our good. I believe that, even if He takes action long after I think He should have. Mary and Martha learned that Jesus could fix anything on His timetable...even bring back their brother, Lazarus, from the dead. I *can* wait on the Lord.

Reflection

In your anger do not sin; when you are on your beds, search your hearts and be silent (Psalm 4:4).

Dear God, this waiting game is tough. It's not fun. In fact, it's just plain hard sometimes. Did I misread You? Or did I hear You plainly, but it's going differently than I expected? The answers probably don't matter. What matters is how I respond to You, regardless of what is going on. May I walk with You and listen to You all the days of my life.

Promises, Promises!

7

Comfort Zone

Gerry and her husband, Ken, browsed a gift shop during a recent trip. They broke out laughing the moment they saw this plaque: If you want breakfast in bed, you'll have to sleep in the kitchen!

It reminded Gerry of their friends Bob and Judy. Bob's idea of a great way to start the day is for his wife to serve him breakfast in bed. Judy's idea of a great way to start the day is for Bob to take her out for breakfast. As each one waits for the other to satisfy his or her need, nothing gets done.

"I almost bought the plaque for Judy to give to Bob," Gerry commented. "But I thought better of it. If I did that, then I'd probably have to give Bob 20 bucks to take Judy out for breakfast. I decided against both. It's really not my place to jump into the middle of their muddle. After all, I don't appreciate people getting into my business."

Instead of focusing on others, Gerry decided to focus on her husband and find out more about what he'd like from her—the things that made him happy and content. *When he expresses a special need for support or love or affection or even breakfast in bed, why fight it? Why not just meet it?* she decided.

Jesus is the perfect model for such behavior. In John 10:10, He says, "I have come that they may have life, and have it to the full."

And in Psalm 37:4, the writer reminds us to "delight yourself in the LORD and he will give you the desires of your heart."

If a perfect God is eager to comfort and encourage inadequate human beings with His good gifts, how can I want less for those I love, even if it costs me a bit of my comfort? Gerry walked out of the gift shop that day with a new resolve: to *listen* for the desires of her husband's heart and to do what she can to meet them.

"It's been working for me too," Gerry shared later. "When I comfort the one I love with the grace and peace that have been given to me, I am a happy and blessed woman."

Gerry and Ken feel closer than ever—and sometimes they even enjoy breakfast in bed. Each one takes a turn being chef and waiter for the day.

Reflection

May your unfailing love be
my comfort (Psalm 119:76).

Lord, You showed the way—all the way to Calvary. You put Your own comfort aside to provide eternal assurance for me. And when You returned to Your heavenly Father, You sent the Comforter to counsel and guide me and to remind me of everything You taught. Thank You for anticipating what I need and for providing it in every way as I walk and talk with You along life's highway.

8

Couch Potato

Millie and Ron decided to run errands on Tuesday morning. They each had a gift certificate for a haircut from their neighbor Jan, a hairdresser. After leaving that shop they spotted Save-a-Lot across the street, where everything in the store is discounted. They walked over and went in. Millie went up one aisle with the shopping cart while Ron went down another with a basket. She gathered boxes of crackers and cookies. Ron loaded up on cherry soda and his favorite brand of potato chips—the one that earned him the nickname "couch potato" from Millie. He chuckled as he picked up three bags. He did love to munch chips and drink cherry soda while sitting on the sofa watching TV.

The two met in the back of the store and decided the sale price on paper goods was worth taking advantage of. They stocked up on paper towels, paper napkins, and toilet paper.

With basket and cart bulging, they headed for the checkout counter. Ron reached into his back pocket, and then clutched Millie's arm so tightly his knuckles turned white. "My wallet. It's gone!" He set the basket on the floor and dashed up and down the aisles, certain he must have dropped it somewhere. That didn't make sense because he'd had no reason to take it out until he was ready to pay for the purchases, but that didn't slow him down.

Millie stepped aside and let the other customers take her place. Her heart pounded as she thought about what this would mean: calling the credit card companies, Ron getting a new driver's license, making a list of all the missing items—if they could even remember them. What a drag! Then Millie was mad—hopping mad. This forgetfulness was happening much too often these days. First a misplaced watch and then car keys and a prize coffee cup and now this—their cash and Ron's wallet.

"Dear God," she prayed, "what's up? Is there a message here we just aren't getting? Please send help ASAP. I'd rather not make a second trip."

Just then Millie remembered she had their checkbook in her purse. She'd put it there the day before to pay a neighbor for some carpentry work he'd done for them.

As Ron strode to the counter breathing hard and wringing his hands, Millie took him by the arm and whispered, "We'll be all right. I have the checkbook."

"But what about my wallet? My life is in it—every card that matters. What if someone gets hold of it?"

Millie ushered them through the checkout stand after writing the check and led her husband to the car. "Your life's in the Lord, not in your wallet," she reminded him. "Wait and see what God will do."

They drove home and Ron dashed into the house, ready to make the calls necessary to cancel their credit cards before someone could use them. As he reached for the phone, he noticed a familiar lump of bent brown leather on the kitchen sideboard—the "lost" wallet. "Hallelujah!" he exclaimed.

Then it dawned on him that he had taken it out just before they left to retrieve the haircut coupons. He'd forgotten to put it back into his pocket.

All was well. He hadn't lost his marbles—just his wallet, and that only temporarily. As he leafed through the billfold, he saw a scripture card he hadn't looked at in a long time: "We live by faith, not by sight" (2 Corinthians 5:7).

Reflection

Praise the LORD, O my soul, and forget not
all his benefits (Psalm 103:2).

*Lord, what a timely reminder, especially when I catch myself
living by sight and not by faith. I make foolish mistakes that
shake me up, but nothing rattles You. Thank You for doing
for me what I can't do for myself.*

9

God's Freebies

Everywhere we look there are offers for free stuff—from a dozen eggs if I spend $25 on groceries to free interest and no sales tax if I purchase a $500 sofa or living-room carpeting. I can get free air miles if I fill out an application for a credit card and a free "second" kitchen gizmo if I pay for the first one...and the additional shipping charge to mail the "free" gizmo. Thanks, but no thanks.

Marketing pitches are cool, clever, and often low-key—so low, in fact, that merchants have dug into our pockets and purses faster than a mole can dig a hole. Then the boxes and bags arrive at our front doors and we wonder what's in them. We slit the tape and plow through the Styrofoam popcorn with anticipation because we've forgotten what we ordered.

But God's promises for free stuff are eternal and authentic. We don't have to do anything to receive them except open our hands and hearts. Here are just a few of His amazing gifts.

> *Rest:* "Come to me, all you who are weary and burdened, and I will give you rest" (Matthew 11:28).

> *Love:* " 'Though the mountains be shaken and the hills be removed, yet my unfailing love for you will not be shaken nor my covenant of peace be removed,' says the LORD, who has compassion on you" (Isaiah 54:10).

Security: "Do not be afraid, little flock, for your Father has been pleased to give you the kingdom" (Luke 12:32).

Parenting: "I will be a Father to you, and you will be my sons and daughters" (2 Corinthians 6:18).

Peace: "Peace I leave with you; my peace I give you" (John 14:27).

Assurance: "Even to your old age and gray hairs I am he, I am he who will sustain you" (Isaiah 46:4).

Consider the promises of God, and then look at the lures of the world. Only the Lord can give you contentment here and eternal life hereafter. So keep on walkin' with Him!

Reflection

What I have said, that will I bring about; what I have planned, that will I do (Isaiah 46:11).

Dear God, I accept Your free gift of salvation and Your assurance of love and protection. You made me, and You will never desert me. Thank You!

10

Ho! Ho! Ho! Santa

Yolanda and her grandson Jacob chatted in the car as she drove him to soccer practice one day in September. Jacob didn't usually burst into song, but this day he was eager to share a new piece of music he'd learned at school.

"Grandma!" he said with excitement. "Wanna hear a new Christmas song I learned today?"

Yolanda was surprised the teacher was introducing holiday music so soon. Why Labor Day had just passed, and they had Halloween and Thanksgiving to think about next. But she didn't want to discourage her grandson. "Sure," she said. "Let's hear it."

Jacob sat up straight, cleared his throat, and belted out, "Ho, ho, ho, Santa. He died to save us from our sins. Ho, ho, ho, Santa. He died to save both you and me."

Yolanda furrowed her brow and looked at her grandson. This was one of the strangest Christmas songs she'd ever heard. And it was theologically incorrect, to boot! Hmmm. "You sang that really well, Jacob," she responded.

She swung into the parking lot next to the soccer field. Jacob got out and headed toward his team. Yolanda decided to call Jacob's mother to suggest she speak to the teacher about the song. After all, Jacob attended a Christian school. Just as she picked up her cell phone to dial, it suddenly hit her. "Hosanna!" she exclaimed "I'll bet Jacob heard the Ho! Ho! part and thought the rest of the phrase was Santa. Ho! Ho! Ho! Santa, instead of Ho-ho-hosanna!" She had a good laugh as she got out to watch the practice.

Reflection

Those who went ahead and those who followed shouted, "Hosanna!" "Blessed is he who comes in the name of the Lord!" (Mark 11:9).

God, I must surely cause you to smile sometimes with my little foibles and follies. And yet You love me with an everlasting love, always wanting the best for me. You're ever ready to bless my efforts even when I fall short or don't hear things just right. Thank You for loving me.

11

Straight Scoop

Pat took her grandson and granddaughter for ice cream one day. It's one of their favorite outings. Hers too. "It's fun to watch them roam back and forth in front of the glass freezer, pointing at the various colors and flavors before making their final selection," she said with a smile. "Sometimes even then the choice they make is not final. They change their minds, which sometimes works in their favor. I allow them two scoops. One's plain like chocolate or vanilla, and the other is special—like bubble gum or mint chip.

"The expressions on their faces as they dive into the dish with a spoon or bite into the tall mound on a cone is delicious in itself. Pure delight! They're ready to enjoy themselves, and when they're finished, they wipe the creamy droplets from their lips and sigh out loud.

"'Thanks, Granny. That was yummy,' or 'Thank you for the ice cream. It was really good,' fill my soul and ears. I sit back in pleasure, loving our sweet time of interaction."

The bits of conversation Pat and her grandchildren share and the advice they trade make their small troubles melt away as they give each other the straight scoop.

Such outings turn our attention to God and His delight in us as we walk with Him day by day. Through the ups and downs He is here to guide and direct us. And when we're hot and weary, flustered or frustrated about some irritant, He invites us to relax and give Him the straight scoop about our lives. He wants to hear from our lips what's on our minds.

Sometimes we talk to Him over a cup of tea. Other times we chat with God during a walk in the park, or on a hike in the hills, or as we sit in traffic on the freeway. He's ready to take it all in as we let it all out.

Reflection

You have made known to me the path of life; you will fill me with joy in your presence, with eternal pleasures at your right hand (Psalm 16:11).

Lord, thank You for taking me on little outings with You— whether a walk in the park, a ride on a highway, a jaunt to the store, a visit with a friend, or a time-out to enjoy a scoop of ice cream and a few minutes of rest. Walkin' with You is the best!

Handiwork

Clean behind the sofa. Paint that room. Organize the hall closet. The list of "I don't wannas" goes on and on. But when you've taken care of yourself first, these items are less debilitating. You may find that you actually look forward to ticking them off your list. My neighbor Marvin told me the best time for him to do chores is after he plays golf on Saturday. "I come home in a pleasant frame of mind—even if I didn't play well."

For over a year my husband and I put off repainting the interior of our home. It seemed too big a job for us and too costly to hire someone else. Then one day Charles poked his head into my home office and said, "If it's okay with you, I'm going to take off the guest bathroom wallpaper today. There's no going back once I do, so what do you say?"

I gulped and then agreed.

"This is great," he said a day later as he mounted the ladder and ran a paint roller across the ceiling. "I'm already thinking how beautiful it's going to look."

Two weeks later both guest and master bathrooms were finished and looked as beautiful as Charles had predicted. The new paint, updated plumbing and wall fixtures, and pretty matching accessories were very inviting.

Painting might not be for you, but you probably have something that needs doing. As Theodore Roosevelt said so well, "Do what you can, with what you have, where you are." The Lord will take care of the rest.

Reflection

But as for you, be strong and do not give up, for your work will be rewarded (2 Chronicles 15:7).

Lord, why is it the things I don't want to do are often the very ones that improve my life—and not just in the natural realm but in my spirit as well? I procrastinate in praying. I put off sitting quietly in Your presence. I often ignore Your nudging until You break through. When I finally focus on You, everything falls into place. I am peaceful, content, joyful, and, most important, grateful to You.

13

Boom! Boom! Boomer!

I remember a time when Boom! Boom! was the sound of my brother and his buddy playing war with their toy guns. Now it refers to a whole group of people called "boomers" born between 1946 and 1964. I missed this target by eight years. The more appropriate chant for me is Pow! Pow! Power! An investment counselor told me recently that based on my current age (68), I have a life expectancy of 110. With that in mind I'm just a bit past middle age. Wouldn't you agree *that's* a powerful position to be in? Cruise lines, investment brokers, physicians, travel agents, car salespeople, retirement village developers, and time-share operators are all after me and the big bucks they assume I have.

Then there are the vendors who think my "real" age is what matters. They assume I live on a fixed income, and I see no good reason to tell them otherwise. These compassionate individuals offer me discounts on movie tickets every afternoon, hamburgers and fries for half price on Tuesdays at Dinette Don's, a free breakfast at the Senior Center every Friday morning, a low-priced concert ticket for the local symphony (if I have it in me to climb to the rafters for a seat), and free lemonade and cookies if I stop by the bank on Monday afternoons instead of Friday afternoons when all the earners are cashing paychecks.

Ah yes, I'm into Pow! Pow! Power! And I'll keep right on enjoying these powerful benefits till I'm 110!

Reflection

Then maidens will dance and be glad, young
men and old as well. I will turn their mourning into
gladness; I will give them comfort and joy instead
of sorrow (Jeremiah 31:13).

Lord, thank You that as I walk with You I have all the power I need. Even in the tough times You turn sadness into joy and provide special discounts to honor my age!

Forgive and Forget

14

Funny You
Should Ask

Myrna pulled out her collapsible grocery carrier from the front closet, reached for her cane and jacket, and then walked out to her car. The cane was in her way as she juggled jacket, purse, and carrier, so she placed it on top of the car until she could empty her hands. She made a point of telling herself not to forget the cane. She knew people who'd put items on the roof of their cars and then driven off with them still in place. "How careless," she mused. "It takes just a bit of concentration, that's all. We're all in too much of a hurry."

She arrived at the grocery store and reached for her cane in its usual spot beside her purse on the floor of the passenger seat. It wasn't there! She panicked. Then it hit her. She had put it on the roof, and by now it had surely fallen off. "So much for concentration!" she scolded herself. "Now what?"

Without her cane she was vulnerable to falling. It was probably rolling around in the middle of the street *somewhere*. But where? She considered retracing her route and going back home. Maybe somebody saw it fall off and had tried to call her since she'd had the good sense to tape her name and phone number to the side of it. Making her decision, she started the car.

As she waited for the stoplight at the exit to the parking lot, a gracious gentleman honked and pointed to the rooftop. "Is that your cane?" he shouted through his open window.

"Funny you should ask," she called back. "I was just going to look for it."

The light turned green, and Myrna slowly pulled over to the side of the road, hoping this last bit of movement hadn't sent the cane rolling onto the street.

What a relief! The cane had slid against the edge of the luggage rack, which kept it from falling off the car. Myrna retrieved the item and held it over her head, not caring who was watching as she pointed heavenward and whispered, "Thank You, Lord."

How often God saves us from our small and large oversights, mistakes, bloopers, and sins. He is always looking out for us and is there to help us retrieve what we have lost—whether a book, a wallet, or a cane...and even our faith and hope in times of trial. We serve a great God who cares for us in big and small ways, in things of the world and in matters of eternity.

Reflection

Cast all your anxiety on him because
he cares for you (1 Peter 5:7).

God, You look out for me each day in every way. What would I do without Your love and care? I am helpless without You. May I stay as close to You as a chick to a hen every moment of the day.

15

Fallin' for Jesus

Pastor Paul completed his sermon and scanned the crowd. He was moved by the sea of faces in front of him. Some men and women appeared hopeful, others peaceful, and still others concerned. He knew what to do in that moment: Give an altar call for those in need of the touch of God.

"Today, I'd like to offer an opportunity to anyone ready to know God personally through the saving grace of Jesus Christ to come forward to receive prayer. Members of our prayer team are waiting to pray with you as you make your confession of faith or reaffirm your commitment."

The pianist played softly as men and women walked up the aisles and stood in front of the church, heads bowed. It was an inspiring moment, the kind that filled Paul with humility and gratitude for his call to the ministry.

Doris and her husband, Greg, went forward. They had pledged their faith in Christ years before, but that day they were moved to renew their commitment to Christ and to one another. The altar was crowded. They found a place where they could kneel and pray together.

After Doris prayed, she stood up and caught her heel on the step. Unable to catch herself, she fell backward—right into the lap of a handsome young man sitting in the front row. Greg rose as well, filled with the joy of his recommitment to Doris—only to find his wife sitting in another man's lap.

The solemnity was broken as smiles and laughter rippled across the sanctuary.

Pastor Paul took the pulpit in the nick of time. "Lord," he prayed aloud, "'Your words have supported those who stumbled; you have strengthened faltering knees.'" He rolled his eyes and chuckled. "And for those of you taking notes, the passage is from Job 4:4."

Reflection

He guards the course of the just and protects the way
of his faithful ones (Proverbs 2:8).

Lord, how faithful You are. When I walk with You I am safe, even when I stumble and fall. You reach out and put me on my feet again so I can keep walkin' with You.

16

Wishful Thinking

Marcy and her friend Dotty offered to prepare a main dish for the annual fall church potluck. They were assigned lasagna. But they disagreed about which of them had the best recipe. Marcy was the more verbal of the two, so she pressed her point...and pointed her finger while doing so. "Whole grain pasta, feta cheese, spinach, and sautéed carrots make mine what it is. You have to try it to see what I mean. It's the best!"

Dotty shrugged and clasped her cookbook to her chest. "Have it your way, Marcy," she said, eyes lowered. "But I like traditional lasagna, and I think most people do."

"It's going to look pretty odd to have two different types in the buffet line when we're supposed to be a team."

Dotty raised her voice. "I'm more comfortable making the kind I'm familiar with."

Marcy threw up her hands and stomped to the door of the church kitchen. "I don't know what to do with you sometimes. You can be so stubborn!" Marcy planted her hands on her ample hips. "We need to be of one mind on this."

Dotty broke into giggles. "We *are* of one mind," she said, laughing so hard she couldn't control herself. "We agree that we can't agree."

Marcy sighed and then smiled. "You're right," she said softly, a twinkle in her eye. "And I don't want to be disagreeable. How about you share your recipe with me and I'll follow it? Most people prefer traditional lasagna, you know."

Reflection

Come near to God and he will come near to you.
Wash your hands, you sinners, and purify your hearts,
you double-minded (James 4:8).

Lord, why is it so important for me to have my own way, even if it means alienating a good friend or, worse, alienating myself from You? Help me walk with You in agreement and obedience. I want to be of one mind with You when I interact with my brothers and sisters in Christ.

17

Turnip Truck

Grandpa Harvey had only an eighth-grade education, so when his two grandsons finished high school and began planning for college, he realized they had passed him up. He was often embarrassed when they got into conversations that were over his head, especially when they discovered history. That was one subject he knew little about. When they got to talking about this war and that one, he got so confused he was afraid they might think he was good for nothing but driving a turnip truck. He wasn't ashamed of his farming background, but it was true that he'd spent more time in the fields than he had in a schoolroom.

He recalled a few dates and phrases, such as "Remember the Alamo," although he couldn't recall what it stood for. And he knew that 1620 was the year the Pilgrims landed at Plymouth Rock—or was it? He scratched his head a few times when the boys got into anything he didn't recognize. He wished he'd had the advantages they had. But he didn't, and that was that. He tried to play along and look interested when they shared facts.

One summer he and the boys and their parents took a trip to Washington, D.C.—a first for the entire family. Grandpa Harvey was pretty excited about this adventure. He had always wanted to see the White House, the Washington Monument, and the Lincoln

Memorial. And he'd heard about the Smithsonian Natural History Museum.

"This'll be my chance to brush up," he told Jeb and Kurt. "Maybe I'll catch up to you two history wizards," he joked.

"Way to go, Grandpa," said Kurt. "We'll all learn something, I'm sure."

On the third day of their week, the family set out for the Smithsonian. They moved from one exhibit to another, stopping here and there to chat about what they saw and discussing what they'd do next.

Jeb tapped his grandfather on the shoulder. "I'm really interested in finding the section with Greek and Roman artifacts," he said. "How about you?"

Grandpa didn't know anything about either one, but it sounded fine to him. "Sure!" he said. "Let's go." He was ready to learn something new. Everyone agreed they'd go together. They stopped at an intersection to read the signs so they'd head in the right direction. They had three choices.

Grandpa Harvey wanted to help in the decision-making, so he turned to the family and grinned with confidence. He remembered something he had learned years ago. Now was the time to show 'em what he knew. "Appears to me you can take any one of the three," he said with a glint in his eye. "Don't all roads lead to Rome?"

Jeb and Kurt burst out laughing. "Hey, Grandpa, you know more than we thought you did!"

Grandpa winked and led the family down the right road—straight to the Roman history exhibit!

Reflection

As the Scripture says, "Anyone who trusts in him will never be put to shame" (Romans 10:11).

Lord, how easy it is to be embarrassed by my lack, whatever it might be: education, money, prestige, intelligence, appearance. But You don't measure me by any of these. You delight in me just as I am because You created me for Your pleasure. Let me put my trust in You alone and hold my head high as we walk together.

18

Sorry State

Silly me.
Couldn't help it.
Pardon me.
O dear!

Most of us have uttered such empty phrases or heard others express them to us. At the most they're lame; at the least they're insulting. Sincere apology over a sin against someone else takes more than a quick phrase and a fast exit. It requires us to humble ourselves before another person and truly *get* the hurt and pain we inflicted. Then it's up to us to repair the damage the best way we can by the grace of God.

I was reminded of this recently when my two-and-a-half-year-old grandson, Miles, asked for his treat after using the potty like a big boy. The customary reward was a couple of chocolate chips. I gave him three, and he closed his little hand around them. He then asked me to put them in a cup the way his mommy does.

I popped the chips into a blue plastic cup and handed it to him. He asked for more. I gave him a couple extras. He asked for more again, and I said, "No, not just now. That's enough for today."

He stomped to the sink and turned the cup upside down, sending the chocolate chips into the drain. He stood his ground and pouted. I was shocked by this unexpected behavior.

"That wasn't nice," I said. I went about my business.

He followed me around the kitchen pulling on my pant leg and making ugly faces and weird grunts at me. I didn't recognize this side of a boy who is usually sweet and joyful. I ignored his attempts to taunt me and continued emptying the dishwasher.

Suddenly he left the room and joined his sisters watching television. Then back he came, asking for yogurt with chocolate chips on top.

"No. You hurt me when you threw the chocolate chips in the sink. I need to hear you're sorry before we can be okay with one another."

He left again. Then a moment later he returned and in his big boy voice he apologized: "Grammy, I'm sorry I got mad at you. And I'm sorry I dumped the chips in the sink."

I bent down to his level and reached out to him. "I forgive you."

We hugged each other, and he helped me dish up the yogurt.

When his mother returned later that night he was quick to tattle on himself. "But I told Grammy I was sorry," he added.

His mother sat forward. "Then what happened?"

"She said, 'I forgive you.'"

"Now it's all better, right?" asked his mom.

Miles nodded and went off to play, a little wiser I hope. He learned what it meant to hurt someone with his anger and defiance, and I learned to ask for a well-deserved apology. Then we both discovered together the healing power of making up with forgiveness and a hug.

It's that way with God, too. He's quick to forgive when we apologize and repent in earnest. If you have something heavy on your heart, go to the Lord and confess. He'll fill your cup to overflowing with love and forgiveness. Then you can move on fully restored.

Reflection

Now I am happy, not because you were made
sorry, but because your sorrow led you
to repentance (2 Corinthians 7:9).

Lord, too often I behave like a self-centered toddler, hanging on to my position, my conviction, my wants despite how they affect other people. Please help me be quick to apologize, to repent, and to forgive so I can be right with You and with the other person.

19

Goose River

Lorna's five-year-old granddaughter, Rosie, loved to dance. She told her grandma she felt like a fairy princess whenever she put on her fancy dress, shiny toe shoes, and the sparkling tiara that Lorna had bought for her birthday.

"I knew she was probably too young to sit through an entire professional ballet," said Lorna, "but still I wanted to introduce her to some of the world's most beloved stories in dance. I bought her a set of DVDs to enjoy. She could watch as little or as much as she was able. And this gift would be something to remember me by. I was a dancer in my younger years."

Lorna was taken by surprise, however, to find out that Rosie took to the performances more than she expected. One evening when Lorna had Rosie for an overnight, the little girl begged her grandma to watch a favorite ballet before she went to bed.

"It's a bit late for an entire DVD," Lorna said, as she glanced at the clock and saw that it was already past Rosie's bedtime.

"Oh please, Grandma!" Rosie begged. "Just five minutes, okay?"

Lorna relented. "All right. A few minutes…as long as you're in your jammies first. Which one do you want?" she called while Rosie was in the guest room changing her clothes.

"*Goose River,*" Rosie replied.

Lorna was perplexed. She asked for a description of the movie from every possible angle, trying to figure out which ballet Rosie was talking about. Certainly Lorna had never heard of *Goose River*.

Rosie was also clearly perplexed. "Why don't you know when you're the one who gave me the DVD?" She walked into the den, slapped her thighs, and frowned. "You know, Grandma. The Barbie movie, you know...the pretty girls twirl around and all the birds..."

Lorna chuckled to herself. Of course! Rosie wanted to watch *Swan Lake*. After Lorna pulled herself together, she set up the DVD player and sat down beside Rosie to watch their favorite ballet—whose name is now *Goose River*...at least in *their* minds.

Reflection

They send forth their children as a flock;
their little ones dance about (Job 21:11).

Lord, walkin' with You sure ain't for wimps. It not only takes patience and courage, but humility too—a virtue that is so evident in the heart and mind of a child—and so difficult to hang on to as an adult. Help me, O God, to live once again in wonder and imagination.

20

Hobnobbing

I shop for some of my groceries at Nob Hill Market. Sometimes I refer to it as Snob Hill because the prices are a bit higher than at Save-a-Lot, but I love the atmosphere, the wide selection of organic produce, and the many familiar health-food brands that I favor.

This week I pulled into the parking lot in front of the store, in a hurry as usual. I didn't make a note of the space I chose. I simply dashed in, bought more than I came for (what else is new!), and rushed through the checkstand. As I wheeled my cart out the front door, a young man headed me off.

"May I help you to your car?" he asked.

I smiled but waved him off. "It's okay. I can manage. Only two bags. No problem."

He took the cart right out of my capable hands.

"I insist. Besides, I like getting out in the fresh air."

I tried to talk him out of it, but he'd have none of my persuasive chatter. Then my heart pounded! *Where did I park? Darn!* If only I'd stop and pay attention this wouldn't happen so often. I was caught. As the man waited for me to direct him to my car, I admitted my memory lapse.

"Good," he said. "It will take longer. I can enjoy being outside on this beautiful day." Then he winked and nudged me with a shoulder. "Is that why you didn't want me to help you out?"

"No," I lied. "I just didn't want to take you away from your work."

He smiled knowingly. I guess he'd heard that line before from other grayheads like me.

"What does your car look like?" he inquired.

Look like? It looks like it's lost—that's what!

I pasted a smile on my face. "Gray, like my hair. A wagon with a rack on top."

He spotted it and in minutes he packed my bags in the trunk. My face turned from red back to white, and I was on my way. *And I thought being a baby boomer was tough,* I thought. *Slipping into elderly isn't all that great! No wonder I have no trouble writing for the over-50 crowd. All I have to do is live my life, take a few notes, and presto, I have a book. My books* Help, Lord! I'm Having a Senior Moment *and* Gettin' Old Ain't for Wimps *have each sold more than 100,000 copies so I know I'm speaking to somebody out there. Is it you? If you're too young to relate now...your time is coming. Get ready!*

Reflection

They will still bear fruit in old age,
they will stay fresh and green (Psalm 92:14).

Lord, thank You for showing me that even though I'm getting old, I will stay fresh and green if I keep bearing fruit and walkin' with You.

Wit and Wisdom

21

Mommy Moment

One evening after Erin's two daughters were asleep, she stayed up late to read and enjoy the quiet. Suddenly the phone rang.

"I grabbed the receiver. When I heard Mom's voice I was worried," Erin shared. "She doesn't call me late at night. I immediately asked what was wrong."

Her mother assured her there was no emergency but asked if she had time to talk.

"I told her I did," Erin said. "Mom's voice was quiet and sounded a bit nervous. Then *I* felt nervous. *What is she calling for?* Mom had been at my house the week before, and we'd had a marvelous time. My girls, ages seven and two at the time, love her so much."

"Honey," her mom said, "I think you're a wonderful mother. It's obvious you love the girls and work hard to make their lives sweet and secure."

Uh, oh, Erin thought. *This is how someone begins a criticism.*

"Mom conveyed in a gentle tone that she'd observed I was very impatient and sharp with my oldest daughter."

"I debated telling you," her mother added, "because I didn't want to discourage you."

"She knew how important it is to me to be a good mother," Erin said. "I was devastated by her comment. I had so much pride in being a gentle, encouraging, intuitive mom. I felt instantly defensive. But Mom isn't a critical person, and she would only tell me something like this for my benefit. I began to cry. I knew what she was saying was true."

Erin thanked her mother for her courage in calling her. "Mom prayed for me and told me she loved me. I hung up the phone and sat in silence, praying and reflecting. I asked God to forgive me and to cleanse me. I knew I needed to ask Shevawn for forgiveness too and start fresh.

"I went to her right then. She was asleep so I climbed into bed with her and woke her gently. When she fully awakened I explained things as clearly and simply as I could.

"She admitted there were times when she felt I was angry or 'fast' with her. I held her close and asked for her forgiveness. She melted in my arms and forgave me totally. We stayed up talking in the dark. Shevawn thought it was pretty special to be up in the middle of the night with me! We prayed together and fell asleep."

When Erin woke, she felt renewed and refreshed, ready to mother her girls with tenderness—by God's grace.

"There are really two *mommy moments* in this story," Erin pointed out. "The intimate moment when my faithful mother spoke the truth in love, and the tender moment of confession and forgiveness with my lovely Shevawn."

Reflection

Create in me a pure heart, O God, and renew a stead-
fast spirit within me (Psalm 51:10).

God, what a relief to know I don't have to be a mom on my own. I have Your wisdom, Your grace, Your gentleness, Your strength to guide me. Thank You!

22

Fuddy-duddy

Therese remembers her mother requiring that she keep her room and her belongings in order when she was a teenager. "I had to make my bed, put my clothes away, and return games, books, and records to their proper places at the end of each day. Mom often entered my room unexpectedly, and if things were a mess she'd roll her eyes and point heavenward. 'Well, I'll give you this. You have a neat ceiling. Now let's see if you can bring the rest of the room up to that high standard,' she'd say.

"I didn't think it was funny then. I thought she was being sarcastic. But when I think of it now, I laugh."

Therese said she resisted her mother every step of the way. "I'd make hateful faces when she wasn't looking. And I made up names for her when I was really mad. My favorite was fuddy-duddy. I'd often mouth the words, *You old fuddy-duddy!* and then hope she couldn't read my lips—or my mind."

Today Therese is 72. She winces as she talks with her friends about this incident. "Mom had my best interest in mind," she admitted. "I give thanks now for what she taught me and expected of me. I'm a pretty orderly person to this day, and my life is a lot smoother because of it."

I chuckled as I listened to Therese's story. I remember thinking my mom was a neatnik because she too had high standards for me when I was growing up. But now I too am grateful because my home and life are pretty well organized. I can lay my head on my pillow at night without worrying about what I did or didn't do with this or that.

I wonder if God gave us mothers and fathers to show us a bit of His character? We have the opportunity each day through them, and long after they're gone, to do what God expects of us—from the mundane (taking care of ourselves and our stuff) to the memorable (serving others joyfully, leaving them better off for having been with us).

Still, there are those days when we are stuck on our needs and ourselves more than on what God wants and needs from us. How tempting it is then to whisper behind His back, "You ol' fuddy-duddy!" But then we feel ashamed that we resisted His wise counsel and loving grace.

Walkin' with God sure ain't for wimps. It's for people who want to glorify Him in everything they think, say, and do...for those willing to step up to the high standards He sets for us.

Reflection

I press on toward the goal to win the prize
for which God has called me heavenward
in Christ Jesus (Philippians 3:14).

God, please help me see beyond what my human eyes can see. I want to be more aware of using my life to glorify Your name through unselfish behavior.

23

Bread and Water

My mother-in-law, Ada, enjoyed telling our family about an incident early in her marriage. Her young husband, Charlie, made life difficult for her in the kitchen. "No one can cook like my mother..." he often said.

"Can you believe it?" Ada commented. "He actually liked his pork chops cooked until they resembled old shoe leather. I decided to fix him," she added with a glint in her soft blue eyes. "Instead of arguing and defending myself, I enrolled in a cooking school. I was only 17 when we married, so I figured I had a few things to learn. That marked a turning point in our relationship. I became a good cook, and he became a grateful eater."

One night after finishing her cooking classes, Ada served pork chops, sauerkraut, and homemade applesauce. Charlie cut into the meat and asked what kind it was. He didn't recognize the plump meat that was cooked to perfection. He'd been used to the flat, fried chop he'd had to chase around the plate with his knife and fork just to get a bite.

"We both laughed at that one," Ada shared. "And over the years, when I asked what he'd like for dinner he always responded the same way: 'How about pork chops—the way *you* fix them.'"

How do you respond when God wants to serve you a beautiful

meal for your spirit—a cup running over with love, a plateful of peace, a bowl of assurance. Do you receive His gift with thanksgiving and praise? Or do you complain about the portion, the size, the texture, and the manner in which He serves it?

Reflection

You will have plenty to eat, until you are full,
and you will praise the name of the LORD your God
(Joel 2:26).

Today, Lord, I turn to You with gratitude instead of grumbling. I receive from Your gracious hand all the nourishment I need in exactly the way I need it. You are my provider and my provision.

24

Fourteen-Carat Gold

Paula and her young nephew Brandon were out for a walk one sunny afternoon while she visited his family. Brandon stopped suddenly, looked at her, and frowned. "How come you don't have a husband?" he asked. "My mom does."

Paula held up her left hand and pointed to the ring finger. "Someday I'd like to have a husband," she said, "and have a pretty ring right here like your mother has."

"Aunt Paulie, we're having a birthday party for you. Did you know that?"

Paula brightened. "You are? I didn't know anything about it."

Brandon hunched his shoulders. "Oops, I think it was gonna be a surprise."

"That's okay. I'll pretend you didn't tell me." She ruffled his red hair, and the two went on with their walk.

"I know what I'm getting you for a present."

Paula clapped her hands together. "Now I'm curious."

"Do you want a hint? It's something to wear around your neck."

"A pretty necklace? How nice."

"It's called Life Alert," he said proudly. "I saw one on a lady at the doctor's office. She was old too, and Mom said she needed it in case she got sick."

"And you think it would help me?"

"If you had a husband, you wouldn't need it."

"I see." Paula stifled a laugh as she pieced together her nephew's plan for her future. He was only six, but apparently he had taken on the responsibility of looking out for his poor maiden aunt who was 51.

Young people remind us of the important things in life: having a spouse as we grow older and holding on to the banister as we go down the stairs. They even offer to buy us a jar of wrinkle cream so we'll look younger when we meet their friends. As one granddaughter coached her grandmother before going to the beach, "You have nice skinny legs, but the blue things on the back don't look too good. Just cover them with a towel and no one will notice."

Does any of that sound familiar? We bark orders at God as though we're in charge. Here we are giving Him free advice about what to do and not do when we're the kids and He is the parent. Something is wrong with this picture. We should be chuckling on the one hand and turning red in the face on the other. Who are we to dish out commentary about how to run the universe when we can't even run our own lives without His mercy and grace?

Reflection

Then the Almighty will be your gold (Job 22:25).

O Lord, I zip my lips before You and, instead, open my heart to Your Word and Your will in all things. Thank You for being with me all the days of my life.

25

Life Support

The other day while driving on the freeway a large semi passed me on the right. A bumper sticker caught my attention. "Without Trucks America Stops." *But without God, life stops,* I thought. *And a lot more than trucks would be affected.*

Isn't it interesting how self-serving human beings are? In one way or another we believe we're essential—invincible even. But then comes that moment of awareness when we realize we're nothing without the Lord. The moment when life delivers a blow to our health, to our finances, to our relationships, to our egos. Then we're on our knees in a split second, asking God to protect and restore us.

I had such a moment not long ago. I had just finished giving a talk to a group of seniors, and I felt pretty good about it. I was pleased with my outfit, the tone of my voice, and the fact that I remembered everything I wanted to say without relying on notes.

I saw a few women dab their eyes as I shared my life story of how God had rescued me when I was divorced, near financial ruin, and had health challenges. I had also bounced back from feeling small, skinny, and not very pretty as a child.

One woman in particular seemed to take in every word I said. When the event was over, I stood at the door to shake hands and thank the guests for coming. She grabbed my hand, pulled me aside, adjusted her wide-brimmed straw hat, looked both ways, and then leaned in. I didn't know what was coming, but I was interested.

"Honey," she said, sounding like a mother to a teenager. "You may not be the prettiest thing on the block, but you're a darn good speaker." With that she unclasped my hand and slipped through the doorway.

I didn't know whether to smile or sob. But then I remembered that without feedback my speaking career would be over. I need to hear from people so I am able to remain fresh and alert...and humble. I accepted her well-meaning message and came down to earth, where I needed to be.

The world will not stop if I quit speaking, I reminded myself, *any more than America would stop without trucks. But without God and His love, life in all its fullness certainly would.*

Reflection

With humility comes wisdom (Proverbs 11:2).

Lord, as the old Shaker hymn states, "'Tis a gift to be humble, 'tis a gift to be free, 'tis a gift to come down where we ought to be." Thank You for bringing me down to where I ought to be, humbly walkin' with You in all ways always!

26

Picture Perfect

As I walked toward the front door of my condominium one after-noon the sunlight glinted off a beautiful spider web suspended between the iron railing along the walkway and the ceiling. I stopped for a moment to study the intricate work of art. It was delicate, sturdy and large. The homeowner was hunkered down in the center of the web, legs tucked under its body. Snoozing perhaps? Or maybe waiting for its prey to drop in. I greeted the little guy (or was it a gal?) and walked on.

The following day I passed by again, and there in the same spot and in the same position was Susie or Sam Spider, still waiting. "You have such patience!" I exclaimed. "I can learn from you."

The next day the spider was at home again, but this time he or she was busily working the web, walking up and down the thin strands, maybe adding another room. I smiled at the persistence and dedica-tion of this little creature—doing what was meant to be done while waiting for God's provision.

How orderly my life would be if I applied the same skill and commitment. Instead of being impatient and sometimes frantic during a time of uncertainty or pain or change, I could do what's in front of me day by day—from small routines such as cooking and washing clothes and watering my flowers to the greater works of writing and teaching and lending a hand to someone in need.

No time is wasted in waiting. God has a purpose and a plan for each of us, and if He tarries, well, that's the way it's supposed to be for now. We can rest in His promise that He will never forsake us. All that we need, God will supply in Christ Jesus, our Savior and Lord.

Meanwhile, it's our job to keep our webs tidy and ready for what He will bring in His time and in His way. Praise Him for what is here and now...and what is to come.

Reflection

I love the house where you live, O LORD, the place
where your glory dwells (Psalm 26:8).

*Lord, I lift Your name on high. Help me accept this time
of waiting as one of Your many gifts that serve a purpose
in Your divine plan for me and for others who walk with
You.*

27

Help Needed— and Wanted!

I never realized until now (living within ten minutes by car from three of my grandchildren) how many advantages there are to being a grandmother. In case you haven't yet experienced this divine season of life, here's a glimpse into some of what you have to look forward to. As a grandmother you'll have:

» someone to tell you she loves the feel of your hands just when you've noticed how old they look.

» someone to spot the stray hair growing out of your husband's ear so you can pluck it before he goes out in public.

» someone to jump up on the kitchen counter in one bound to reach a bowl or a cup that is too high for you.

» someone to tell you that your shoes are cool, your earrings are just the right color, but your turtleneck shouldn't be tucked in. "You're supposed to wear it over your jeans."

» someone with whom to make cookies, read bedtime stories, skip in the rain, laugh at knock-knock jokes, and fall asleep in front of favorite cartoons.

Being a mother is superb. Being a grandmother is supernal!

Reflection

Whoever welcomes one of these little children in my name welcomes me (Mark 9:37).

Thank You, Lord, for grandchildren. Gettin' old ain't so bad after all—as long as I keep on walkin' with You.

Thorny
Issues

28

On the Go

Marilyn sat in the lobby of a medical center waiting for her return ride to the care facility where she lived. A woman with two young boys trailing behind ran up to her. "Excuse me, ma'am, but do you know where there's a key to the ladies' room? It's urgent!"

"I felt for her," Marilyn told me. "I know what it's like to have a physical need and not be able to meet it right then." At the time all the offices in the small building were closed for lunch so there were no keys available.

Marilyn thought for a moment. Then she remembered one time using an unlocked facility on the second floor. She passed on that information to the woman.

A few minutes later an elderly man with a cane wandered through the lobby looking confused. He asked Marilyn if she knew where to get a key to the men's room. She directed him to the second floor as well. He scurried off, mumbling that he really had to go. Within minutes the woman with the two boys reappeared.

Marilyn looked up from her wheelchair. "Did you have any success?"

"Both are locked," said the woman. "We're going to be in big trouble in a minute." She grabbed the boys' hands and off they went. "Imagine, not one available restroom in this entire building!"

"Lord," Marilyn prayed, "what's a person to do in a case like this? It's enough to make someone angry. It's a doctors' building, for goodness' sake. When we have to go, we have to go! And no one knows that better than older people and young moms with little kids. Banks and restaurants and gas stations these days have locks on the restroom doors and signs that say 'For Customer Use Only.' Watch out for us, Lord."

Marilyn realized she'd have to plan her trips carefully from then on so she wouldn't get caught in that situation. Such a small thing, and yet so important when the need is there. She whispered a prayer for the woman with the two boys and the man with the cane—that God would lead them—knowing He cares for each one of us, including our daily functions.

Reflection

I will give you the keys of the kingdom
of heaven (Matthew 16:19).

God, the keys to Your kingdom are the only ones that really matter. And I don't need to depend on someone in an office building to hand them to me. I don't have to wait in line to use them either. You have given me full access to Your heart and home. How I thank You for that. All of my needs will be met in You.

29

Flower Power

I'm tired of planting flowers that die or succumb to bugs," Les told his wife, Minnie. He shook his head and let out a deep breath. "What do you say we pick out some fake bloomers, and we'll have color all year long without the fuss and financial drain?"

Minnie had wanted pots of living marigolds and geraniums, but she too was ready to call it quits. The couple had spent a lot of money on blooming plants year after year, but they simply didn't last. The next day they headed for Michaels, "The Arts and Crafts Store," and in a few minutes they found four beautiful faux bushes. And they were on sale! The two were thrilled. "We knew this was the answer to our gardening dilemma," asserted Les.

They also purchased a spray bottle of artificial flower cleaner. All they had to do was spritz the blooms and leaves whenever they got dusty, and they'd be as beautiful as ever as soon as they dried. What could be easier? This was their kind of gardening.

Les and Minnie were both happy with this set-up for well over a year. Then one day everything changed. While eating breakfast one morning Minnie looked outside, caught by the strands of blue and gold and orange that broke across the sky as the sun popped up.

"I watched the sunrise in awe," she said, "and then lowered my eyes to avoid the glare. That's when I saw *it*. The tiny head of a marigold pushing its way up from the soil leftover in the pots on our front deck. Attached were several buds about to break into full bloom. I chuckled out loud. *Go, Mari, go!* I thought. It was fighting for its space even though the faux bush took up most of the room.

"Les," she squeaked, "look at this! The marigolds are back, and they appear to be thriving." Minnie couldn't imagine how. She hadn't watered or fertilized or given any thought to them since she threw the last of the bunch out and replaced them with the fake bouquets.

Grace, she thought. *It's God's grace. How else could they survive?*

As Minnie looked closer, the contrast between the genuine and the counterfeit startled her. "The real flower was full of life and power and grit. I could feel it as well as see it," Minnie related. "The imposter was a cheap imitation I had grown bored with because there was no growth and no surprises."

Gosh, Lord, are You trying to tell me something here?

The faux flowers of life are often such a good imitation of the real that we can't tell them apart—until God disturbs the undersoil of our lives and pushes through with grace and guidance, causing us to bloom where we're planted.

Reflection

It will burst into bloom; it will rejoice greatly
and shout for joy (Isaiah 35:2).

Lord, thank You for showing me an important life lesson. To serve You requires that I be real, keep growing even when it's tough, and hold up my head as I push through the hardships of life. Walkin' with You certainly is not for wimps!

30

Bunion Branches

I took a walk through Balboa Park in San Diego last week and stopped at a grove of trees that captured my attention. The trees were *old*, actually older than old. Gnarly limbs and sagging branches with multiple growths stuck out on all sides, but beautiful vibrant green leaves clung to the vines like children to their mother. One tree was lovelier than the next, despite the "bunions." Perhaps their delightfulness resulted from these signs of old age. They'd been pummeled by the elements over many decades, but they had survived and appeared to be proud of it.

That evening as I undressed for bed I looked at myself in the mirror. From head to toe I had some of the same signs as the trees in the park—wrinkles here, sags there, a bunion here, a small growth there. All part of the aging process. None were serious, but most of them were obvious. But then I got to thinking. *If the ancient trees are beautiful, is there a chance that I am still beautiful despite the fact that gravity is winning?* I didn't have to wait long for an answer.

My husband made my day when he sidled up to me as I brushed my teeth. "Not bad lookin' for an older woman," he said. "You're gorgeous to me and always will be."

"Really?"

"Absolutely."

We hugged and kissed and padded our way to bed, slipping between the sheets to cuddle a bit before going to sleep.

Just before nodding off, a Bible verse I had read many times slipped into my mind: "Your beauty should not come from outward adornment....Instead, it should be that of your inner self, the unfading beauty of a gentle and quiet spirit, which is of great worth in God's sight" (1 Peter 3:3-4). Ah! The most encouraging words of all. God loves me and God loves you—just as we are—lumps and bumps and all. Yep, walkin' with God ain't for wimps. It's for people who are all right with themselves—knots, wrinkles, bunions, and all.

Reflection

Flowers appear on the earth; the season of
singing has come (Song of Solomon 2:12).

Thank You, Lord, for loving me as I am and for filling my life with the grace and grit to walk with You without fainting.

31

You Said What?

Darlene picked up the phone. Her pulse jumped as she listened to her husband, Dick, tell her what just happened. A motorcyclist had crashed into his car and was rushed to the hospital.

"Are you okay?" She envisioned her husband covered in blood and gashes from broken glass and twisted metal.

"I'm fine," he said, "but the driver was hurt pretty bad. We'll have to wait and see how he does."

"I'll start praying right away," Darlene promised.

"Yes, do," Dick said. "And pray for me too. Some bystanders are pointing the finger at me even though I didn't have anything to do with it. He hit me from behind."

"Then what's their point?"

"One fella said I caused it because I braked too fast for the motorcyclist to see my red lights in time."

Darlene persisted with questions. She wondered if her elderly husband might be at fault after all. His driving skills lately concerned her. She questioned her husband more.

"Look, dear," he said with irritation, "I didn't hit the driver in front of me. Doesn't that count for something? It means I was driving a safe distance from that person's car."

Darlene backed down. "I'm sorry. I didn't mean to hurt your feelings. I'm jumpy, that's all."

"I know what you mean." Dick breathed hard. "It's in God's hands now. He saw the whole thing." Dick chuckled softly. "He's the only unbiased witness."

Weeks later what Darlene feared came true, only much worse than she had imagined. Dick was charged with vehicular manslaughter. The motorcyclist had died in the hospital.

A year later, during the 10-day trial, Dick and Darlene faced the charges against Dick. He cooperated fully with the attorneys, and the couple wrapped the event in prayer with family and friends.

"There was absolutely nothing we could do on the human plane to affect the outcome of the case," said Darlene. "We were entirely dependent on God's mercy and grace. So we started each day singing His praises and thanking Him for the result that would glorify Him."

The trial ended and Dick was exonerated.

So remember: Whatever you face, don't face it alone. Praise, worship, and give thanks to God. He will not forsake you.

Reflection

But let all who take refuge in you be glad; let them
ever sing for joy. Spread your protection over them,
that those who love your name may rejoice in you
(Psalm 5:11).

Dear God, how You take care of Your people! May I turn to You in praise and thanksgiving every day of my life and not just when things are difficult. A familiar slogan says: When the going gets tough, the tough get going. I'd like to rewrite that. When the going gets tough, the tough get going with praise, worship, and gratitude—clinging to You as You walk with them day by day.

32

Hedging Our Bets

Brad pulled a pen from his jacket pocket and laid it on the desk. He wanted to make a point with the businessman sitting across his desk. "Try to pick it up," he commanded.

Hank reached over and picked it up. He frowned as if to ask, "What's the point?"

Brad read his mind. "The point is that *trying is lying*. You either pick it up or you don't. There's no such thing as *trying*. We either do what we say we're going to do or we don't. It's that simple. I know you can increase your sales numbers."

Hank folded his arms and looked out the window. He turned back to Brad and stated his position. "I don't agree. There are plenty of things in life that are just plain hard. It's not as simple as just doing or not doing. Some actions take time and training."

"You're right. It's not simple," Brad agreed. "But even the most challenging tasks or goals are made up of hundreds of little steps along the way. Each time we have the opportunity to keep our word we choose to do what we say we'll do or we hedge our bets by saying, 'I'll try.' We need to give our all to every endeavor. 'I'll try' should be eliminated from our vocabulary!"

Hank stood up and shook Brad's hand. "Thanks. I think I've got it. See you at the Senior Golf Tourney on Tuesday morning. And I won't *try* to beat you. I will beat you!"

Reflection

Always give yourself fully to the work of the Lord
(1 Corinthians 15:58).

Lord, You could call me a hedger and be telling the truth. I qualify what I'll do by saying "I'll try" much too often. I'll try to read a chapter of the Bible each day. I'll try to pray every night before I go to sleep. I'll try to help my neighbor. I'll try to clean up the clutter in my house. Please help me today to give up trying—and just do what I say I'll do.

33

Choice Morsels

BARNEY'S BEST BREAD. The sign hung over the doorway of the small shop Eleanor had been looking for. It was the new neighborhood bakery everyone was talking about. She couldn't resist the fragrance of fresh-baked bread wafting through the doorway. As she crossed the threshold a little bell jingled. The sign above the counter showed a list of choice morsels: 12-grain, cranberry-nut, multiseed, whole wheat, and dark rye.

"Spread a thick slice with soft creamery butter, bite into it, and you'll think you've died and gone to heaven," Eleanor told me. I savored the thought of the lovely dough and golden spread.

"I took a couple of loaves home with me," Eleanor added, "ready to make a hit with my husband. He immediately dove into two and in seconds he was licking his lips and fluttering his eyebrows a la Groucho Marx. I knew I had scored several points."

But when Eleanor reached for a slice herself, Duffy raised an anxious hand and his brows furrowed. "Easy now. You've been watching those carbs, remember? I'll take that off your hands so you won't be tempted anymore." With that her husband sauntered out of the kitchen and into his cave—the den—bread and butter in hand.

"I was left holding the bread bag," Eleanor complained.

But Eleanor kept her secret to herself—the three slices she'd eaten while driving home from Barney's. "There's always another day to start watching the carbs," she asserted.

Reflection

Then Jesus declared, "I am the bread of life. He who comes to me will never go hungry" (John 6:35).

After the last slice is cut and the crumbs gathered up, there's nothing left but the memory. It might be the bread of today, tomorrow, even the next day—but finally it runs out. Only You, dear Lord, are the bread of life, the one who fills my hungry soul and nourishes my spirit as I walk and talk with You.

34

Dummy Drain

Maggie woke up with one thing on her mind: clean the house before her kids and grandkids came for the weekend. She wanted everything to be spotless—even the fridge. *I'll put the racks in the bathtub, add a splash of ammonia, and soak them in hot water,* she decided.

She turned on the hot water spigot and lowered the refrigerator racks into the tub. She went into the kitchen, and got the bucket and sponge mop she'd set out for cleaning the tile floors. She then moved into the living room, dining room, and den, dusting, spritzing the mirrors and pictures, and finally vacuuming the carpet and sofas.

By then her back was killing her. *A short nap is just what I need,* she thought. Maggie turned on a Bill Powell CD and let the soft piano sounds soothe her mind and spirit as she drifted off to sleep.

She woke with a start. The sound of running water sent a shiver up her spine. She dashed into the bathroom. The tub! Hot water was still running, now over the top, down the sides, and across the floor.

She glanced at the "stupid vent" in the middle of the floor that was slowly draining some of the water. Maggie tossed up a prayer of thanksgiving: "O God, you are so good to me!" She ran to the linen closet and pulled out every towel she could get her hands on.

She sopped up as much water as they could hold and wrung them out in the tub...after releasing the stopper.

This is one way to avoid mopping the bathroom floor, she mused and then broke out laughing. By that point, Maggie needed another nap!

Reflection

The Lord knows how to rescue godly
men from trials (2 Peter 2:9).

Lord, I praise Your name today and every day. When I am weak—and a bit stupid and forgetful—You are strong of mind and spirit. You shower me with love and forgiveness and compassion, which I need today in mega doses.

Money
Matters

35

Penny for Your Thoughts

Barbara and her husband, Hank, are moving to a new city at the end of the month so they're in the process of filing and tossing and getting organized. Now they can't find anything.

Last Saturday Hank tore up his home office looking for a checkbook he was certain he'd seen just days before. Barbara joined the search, which was a mistake.

"I like to implore the help of the Holy Spirit right away and get immediate results," she gushed. "But Hank would rather look by himself first and *then* ask God."

After an hour Barbara and Hank had gone through every cupboard and drawer space in their home but still no checkbook.

Barbara looked Hank in the eye. "Do you think you put it in one of the boxes we're taking in our car instead of a box for the movers? That would make more sense, wouldn't it?"

Hank stared at his wife. "What do you take me for—a dope? Of course it makes more sense, but I told you I already checked the car and it's not there."

They quit looking, but Barbara continued to pray. "I just knew God would put His finger on it and lead us to it. Sure enough, a few moments later I heard a 'whoop' from the other room."

"I found it!"

Barbara hurried to the place where Hank was standing, checkbook in hand.

"It was right here all along," he said, holding out a shoebox. "I just remembered I put a few personal items in this old box to take in the car."

"What a good idea," said Barbara. She closed her mouth before adding another comment, chuckled to herself, and mouthed the words, "Thank You, Holy Spirit."

Reflection

His God instructs him and teaches him
the right way (Isaiah 28:26).

Dear God, You are amazing, and You're mighty patient too. You look after me even when I'm too proud to ask for help. And You soften my heart of judgment against another person when I think I've got all the answers.

36

No Wooden Nickels

Gracie and Harold planned to celebrate their fiftieth wedding anniversary with dinner and dessert at Chez Andre—their favorite restaurant. June 8 was the one day of the year when Harold would spring for a truly special evening. Most of the time he guarded his pennies, nickels, quarters, and dollars like a shepherd guarding a flock of sheep.

"I had to make a strong case every time I suggested a purchase or a vacation or a meal out," Gracie groused.

"I'll think about it," was Harold's standard reply to nearly every request for money.

After more years of this than Gracie could stand, she decided to take matters into her own hands. Whenever Harold stalled with "I'll think about it," Gracie responded, "I'll give you ten minutes, and if I don't hear back by then, I'll assume the answer is yes."

Harold would laugh and look at his watch. "You're on." He welcomed the challenge. However, he usually overlooked the fact that he was getting a bit forgetful in his old age. Two minutes, ten minutes, an hour. They were all about the same to him. Gracie, on the other hand, counted on her husband's forgetfulness. It worked in her favor when she wanted a few bucks for an important purchase.

The one she had in mind for their anniversary was really important.

She approached Harold the morning of June 8. "Honey, can you trust me with a few dollars?"

Harold looked over his coffee cup and muttered, "I'll think about it."

She gave her standard reply. Then Gracie glanced at the kitchen clock: *Ten minutes till yes.*

She cleaned up the breakfast dishes and when the clock read 10:07 she grabbed the checkbook out of the desk drawer and headed for the car. An hour later she returned, giddy with the purchase she'd hidden in the garage.

Harold whirled around in his easy chair. "Where've you been? I must have dozed off."

"Shopping."

"But I'm still thinking about it," Harold complained.

"Your ten minutes was up an hour ago," Gracie said in a sweet voice.

"This better be a good one." Harold pushed himself out of the chair. "Okay, how much did I lose?"

"You lost an old workbench."

Harold hustled out to the garage. There stood a new compact workbench with a matching stool—something he'd always wanted but was too cheap to buy for himself.

Tears welled in his eyes. He turned to Gracie and put his arms around her. "You got me this time," he said and kissed her like he hadn't done for a long time.

"Oh, Harold!" she said. "I just love it when you *think about it!*"

Reflection

Listen carefully to my words; let your ears
take in what I say (Job 13:17).

Lord, when You ask me to do something for my own good, how often I mutter, "I'll think about it." It's embarrassing to admit, but it's true. Today I want to change that behavior. Instead of thinking about what You said, help me simply do it.

37

A Dollar
and a Dream

I love shopping at Dollar Tree. All I need is a dollar and a dream. I can buy facial tissue, cold cereal, a kitchen knife, a box of note-cards, a six-pack of drinking water, a bag of oranges, and a bunch of bananas with a $10 bill and get $3 back. Or I can add a picture frame, a box of cookies, and a large bottle of fruit juice and shoot the entire ten bucks. However I do it, I still come out ahead of shopping at the local grocery store. And I've had an hour or so of fun as well. You can't beat that! Unless, of course, I forget the most important thing of all, which happened to me last week.

I invited my husband to join me and he agreed. We zipped up one aisle and down another, sped around the corners, peered on tiptoes at items on the high shelves, and bent down to examine the clutter on the lowest shelves. I didn't want to miss a bargain. This was my day. I had my list of dreams and plenty of dollars to make them come true. We loaded our cart with goodies—from aftershave to *Zoo Babies*, a picture book for our grandson—and headed to the checkout stand.

I reached into my purse. No ATM card. I poked into my pockets. No spare change. I turned to my husband, palms open. "Can you cover me?" I pleaded.

He let out a deep breath and with a self-satisfied expression reached into his back pocket. "Empty!" he declared. "I didn't bring my money 'cause I didn't plan to buy anything."

We shrugged, half-smiled at the clerk, and apologized for the trouble we caused. I'd left home attached to my dream but arrived unprepared to fulfill it. A small mistake but one I can learn from.

How often we prepare a dream in our hearts but fail to do what it takes to bring it to reality. Like the foolish virgins (Matthew 25:10), we show up without enough oil and then find out that while we went to replenish our supply, the party began and the door of admission shut.

Missing the specials at the Dollar Tree is not a big deal in everyday life, but missing what God has for us because we fail to prepare for His blessings may cost us peace of mind, good health, and harmonious relationships.

With God all things are possible. We can begin again. Ask Him what dream He has for you—a new friend, a lovely vacation, a career opportunity, renewed health. Then prepare to receive it by following His lead, whether it be taking action or sitting still while He goes before you.

Reflection

In the last days, God says, I will pour out my Spirit on all people. Your sons and daughters will prophesy, your young men will see visions, your old men will dream dreams (Acts 2:17).

Dear Lord, my dream for myself is small and insignificant compared to Yours for me. Today, please show me what to do to realize Your dream for my life.

38

Due Credit

Sid had five dollars worth of credit at Hannah's House and Garden. It burned a hole in his pocket. He couldn't wait to return to the store and put it toward some new gizmo for his workshop.

He got to the store and walked up and down the aisles. *A new saw? Maybe. Oh, that weather-stripping looks good. Hey, what about a new set of lights for the front walkway?*

There were too many choices. He rounded the corner into the aisle with garden accessories and there it was—the perfect item. He was so glad he'd come in this morning. A fancy birdbath. He could apply his credit, and that would make it a great deal. *Irene will love this. She's always wanted to attract more birds to our yard.*

Sid lugged the box onto a shopping cart and wheeled it to the checkstand. He pulled out the credit slip and his credit card to take care of the balance. He walked out to his truck, loaded the cargo into the back, and headed home.

He pulled into the garage, and his wife called hello from the side yard where she was weeding and watering the flowerbed. Sid could hardly wait to surprise her. He unpacked the birdbath and scooted it along the walkway. "Surprise!" he shouted.

Irene squealed at the sight of the cute fixture. She took off her sun hat, mopped her forehead, and wrapped her arm around Sid's neck. "Thank you! I love it, and I know the birds will too."

Sid positioned it near their dogwood tree, filled the bowl with water, and stepped back to admire it.

Irene smiled at Sid. She was obviously pleased with the surprise. "By the way, how much did it cost?"

Sid cocked his head and smiled broadly. "It was a steal!"

"Really? On sale?" Irene seemed doubtful that such a beautiful item could be "a steal."

"One hundred dollars out the door," he said, "but I had a credit slip. So we saved."

"How much credit?" She looked wary now.

"Five dollars," Sid boasted.

Irene sank into a nearby lawn chair. "You spent $100 in order to save $5?"

"Don't I get a little credit?" he asked.

"Sorry, Sid," Irene comforted. "I think the store gets the credit for this one!"

Just then a blue jay landed on the edge of the new birdbath, hopped into the water, and fluttered its wings.

Irene turned to Sid. "I take that back. The bird and I are willing to give credit where credit is due. Thank you for this delightful surprise."

Reflection

Look at the birds of the air; they do not sow or reap
or store away in barns, and yet your heavenly Father
feeds them (Matthew 6:26).

Lord, thank You for surprises and delights, for needs and wants. You deserve all my praise and thanksgiving—and all the credit!

39

Pickpocket

Gloria and her husband, Gil, like to tuck a dollar or a bit of change into their grandchildren's pockets now and again. "They love to buy their own ice cream cone or pick up a little toy," Gloria commented. "We didn't have much when we were kids, so we get a kick out of blessing Danny and Laura in this way."

The custom was well established when a younger sister came along. By the time baby Renee was three years old she knew a little about money and what she could do with it. In fact, she kept her grandmother hopping whenever they went grocery shopping together. As they strolled up and down each aisle and packed the cart with food and treats, Renee never failed to remind Gloria, "Before we go you have to pay."

"I guess she thought I was a thief in disguise," joked Gloria.

One day Gil had a roll of quarters and a few single dollars in his jeans pocket. "Who wants a bit of spending money?" he asked while he and the kids took a drive to a nearby mall.

"Me!" shouted eight-year-old Danny.

"Me too!" echoed his younger sister Laura.

"I want some!" squeaked Renee.

Gil wasn't sure the youngest child knew what it meant to have spending money, but he didn't want to leave her out, so he pulled out enough for all three.

He doled out three singles for Danny, three for Laura, and then he counted out 12 quarters for Renee and slipped them into her pocket for safekeeping. Renee, by that time aged four, wrinkled her brow and gave Gil a knowing look. She reached into her pocket, picked out the quarters, and gave them all back.

"What's this about?" Grandpa Gil asked. "You don't want to buy an ice cream or a toy?"

She took a deep breath. "Yes. But, Papa, I only like the green stuff."

Reflection

He who gathers money little by little makes
it grow (Proverbs 13:11).

Lord, oh the wisdom and delight of little children! Even at a young age they are perceptive and wise, yet still they remain innocent. They tell it like it is. May I learn from them in order to draw closer to You.

40

A Dime a Dozen

Lucy was an expert pastry maker. She was known in her community for mango tarts, cappuccino cookies, and chocolate lava cakes. But a real favorite with the young moms and their children were her silk chocolate chip cookies, a recipe handed down from Lucy's mother. Lucy was modest about her talent to the point of embarrassment for her daughter, Janice, who had prodded her mom many times to start a little side business filling orders for her delicacies.

"It'll bring in some cash," Janice said. "And it will give you something meaningful to do now that Dad's gone."

One Saturday Janice dropped in on her mother while Lucy was baking a couple dozen silk chocolate chip cookies to give to a friend who had turned 75. Janice went into her usual song and dance about her mother starting a pastry business.

Lucy wiped her hands on her apron, and then planted her hands on her hips. "No, and that's my final word on the subject," she said.

"Mom, you're being stubborn. You said yourself you could use a little capital. You want to travel and keep up the house. People would be happy to pay you. In fact, you'd be doing them a favor. Where can anyone buy a dozen cookies that compare to yours? Or a truffle cake with the love and care you put into every slice?"

Lucy folded her arms across her chest. "You're persistent, I'll give you that. But I think you're exaggerating my talent because you're my daughter. These cookies are a dime a dozen."

Janice sighed and rolled her eyes. She kissed her mom goodbye and headed out the door. Lucy appreciated her daughter's confidence, but she wasn't about to go into business. She liked giving her goodies to friends and neighbors.

The following week Janice stopped by about the time Lucy was pulling cookies out of the oven. The warm, chocolaty aroma filled the kitchen.

"Hi, Mom. I came by to see if you can spare a dozen cookies. I volunteered to bring dessert to a baby shower this afternoon and forgot about it till now."

Lucy pulled out a plate, filled it with the fragrant cookies, and handed it to her daughter. Janice, in turn, took out her change purse and put a dime on the counter.

"What's this for?" Lucy asked.

"I'm relieved to know you've decided to go into business. Remember last week? You told me cookies were a dime a dozen."

Lucy burst out laughing. She picked up the dime and plopped it into a jar on the counter. "You win!" she said. "Thanks for being my first customer."

Reflection

The worker deserves his wages (Luke 10:7).

Dear Lord, You want me to be generous—not only to others but to myself, as well. It is okay to receive payment for the talent I use and the service I give to others. Looking after myself financially doesn't take away from walkin' with You.

Ice Breakers

41

Bounce Back

Rhoda reached for her cell phone the moment it rang. "Rhoda here."

"And Rudy *here*."

It was her twin brother. Rhoda knew something must be wrong the moment she heard his voice. He never called to chitchat.

"I'm calling about Lou's birthday dinner. I…"

Rhoda jumped in. She knew what was coming, and she didn't want to hear it. They'd been through this nonsense a dozen times before. Rudy always cancelled at the last minute. He had a new excuse every time. She hadn't seen him in two years and three months—she'd kept track.

"I'm disappointed," Rhoda said. "No, I'm not disappointed. I'm hopping mad, and that's the truth. We're family, for Pete's sake! When are you going to get that?"

Rudy was silent on the other end.

Rhoda took the opportunity to keep going. She started with him missing their mom's eightieth birthday umpteen years before, her kids' graduation parties, her daughter Lola's wedding, Cory's baptism, Margaret's piano recital, and much more. She carried on right down to the present, to her husband's eightieth birthday. She finished her

speech and breathed a sigh of relief. *There!* She'd finally said everything she'd been holding back for years.

Silence.

"Well, what do you have to say for yourself?" she asked, breath-
less from her long tirade.

"I mislaid the invitation, and I just called to see what time to be
there," Rudy replied.

Reflection

Why do you look at the speck of sawdust in your
brother's eye and pay no attention to the plank in
your own eye? (Luke 6:41).

*Oh Lord, sometimes I have such a big mouth. I'm so quick
to judge others and so slow to judge myself. Teach me to
listen, to hear, to keep silent, and to give another person a
chance to express himself without my running ahead. I have
so much to learn as I keep living for You.*

42

Go Fish

L oretta's dad, Joe, came to live with her and her husband, Ron, when Joe turned 85. By that age he needed extra help, and Loretta felt more comfortable having him with her than on his own. He was also a big help. He fed the dog and fish, and he kept the flowers in the yard fertilized and watered.

One day at a local fair in town, Joe won a goldfish. He was tickled with his new pet. He took the little fellow home in a plastic bag filled with water. No need for a fishbowl, he decided. He'd just add the new fish to the bowl already on the kitchen counter. But when he saw how aggressive the first fish was toward the new goldfish he went to a local pet store to inquire about this behavior.

"What kind of fish is the first one?" the clerk asked.

"An Oscar," Joe answered.

The clerk laughed. "That explains it." He pointed to the feeding instructions on the tank holding Oscars: "Favorite food—goldfish."

Joe didn't know what was so funny. He knew just what to do to take care of the problem. He thanked the clerk for setting him straight and off he went to the grocery store. He marched right down the aisle displaying crackers and cookies. "Yep, here's just the ticket," he muttered to himself. He picked up two packages of Goldfish crackers, paid for them, and walked home.

115

That night Ron asked Joe if he knew anything about the mush accumulated at the bottom of the fish bowl. Joe was in charge of feeding the fish and cleaning the tank.

"Oh *that*," Joe replied. "I found out at the pet store that Oscars' favorite food is goldfish so I picked up a couple of packages at the market."

Ron jumped up, grabbed a cup, and pulled out the *real* goldfish and put it into a bowl of its own. It was a close call!

Joe scratched his head. He still didn't see what all the fuss was about.

Reflection

Rule over the fish of the sea and the birds of
the air and over every living creature that moves
on the ground (Genesis 1:28).

Lord, sometimes I do the darndest things—even with the best of intentions. It's a good thing there are people around to keep me in line. And even better is the knowledge that You will enlighten my confused thinking with the power of Your Word.

43

Stand Tall

Bonnie felt sensitive about her height from the time she hit 12 and all the other girls began passing her up. She never did catch up. At age 72, she was only 4' 11." Now she feared she might start going the other way, as many older women do. She already looked up to her three grandsons, each one towering at six feet and more.

Her friends teased her about her petite stature. They probably meant well, but meaning well didn't cut it with Bonnie. She dreamed about being 5' 10," walking down a runway in a glamorous outfit, everyone admiring her slim figure and slender good looks. So much for dreams. She missed the runway by several decades and more than 11 inches!

One Monday afternoon Bonnie was feeling especially sorry for herself. In fact, she was having a pity party for one. She sat down with a cup of Rise and Shine tea, but even this happy brew didn't lift her spirit. She was getting old. She was short. Most people over-looked her, and she'd lost confidence in her ability to manage her daily affairs. Life was wearing her down.

A knock at the door jarred her thoughts. She popped up and peeked through the shuttered windows. It was her neighbor and good friend Iris. Bonnie invited her in and the two women sat down for a chat.

"How's it going?" Iris inquired.

That did it. Bonnie's feelings poured out like water from a leaky faucet. Soon she was crying, then sobbing, and finally shaking so badly she couldn't pull herself together.

Iris reached over and took Bonnie's hand in hers. "Come on, Bonnie," she coaxed, "you're just having a bad day. It'll pass. I'll pray for you before I go."

The two spent time in prayer, finished their tea, and then stood up to say goodbye. Bonnie followed Iris to the door.

"I'll leave you with one piece of advice," Iris said. "It never fails to work for me: *Stand tall!*"

Bonnie broke out in tears all over again. "Easy for you," she declared. "You're 5' 7". I'm 4' 11"."

Reflection

Humble yourselves, therefore, under
God's mighty hand, that he may lift you up in
due time (1 Peter 5:6).

Lord, it is so easy to get preoccupied with the standards of the world—youth, beauty, stateliness, height, brawn, grace. But You don't measure my worth by such things. You tell me to humble myself before You—and then You will lift me up to where You want me to be when You want me to be there. I'm waiting on You, O God.

44

Fall on
Your Knees

Garth walked forward at church on Christmas morning after an inspiring service and received Jesus Christ as his personal Savior. His wife, Jeanette, stayed in the pew, blotting the tears that poured down her cheeks. For 40 years she'd been praying for this moment.

"Oh God, how thankful I am for Your mercy and goodness," she prayed as she watched her precious husband make a commitment of faith. Their life together was about to be transformed. She knew it.

Garth returned to the seat next to her and squeezed her hand. His eyes shone and there was a softness around his mouth and chin that had not been there before. She shivered at the sight of this changed man she had shared her life with for so long.

Afterward, in the lobby, longtime friends came forward to congratulate and bless Garth on this important step. He had often accompanied Jeanette to church but had never participated in any of the songs or rituals.

The couple decided to continue their celebration over lunch at Dan's Deli. As they sat in their favorite corner booth, Garth seemed preoccupied and almost sullen. Jeanette feared something was terribly wrong.

She reached across the table and took his hand. "What is it?" she asked.

"I'm worried about something."

"Want to talk about it?" Jeanette felt her heart pound a bit too fast.

"Seems like Christians sing and talk a lot about falling on their knees. It was in one of the Christmas carols this morning, and the elder who prayed with me suggested I kneel so he could lay hands on my head."

"Why is that a problem?" Jeanette asked, curious about this concern.

"With these bum knees," he said, "I'm afraid I'll fall down all right and won't be able to get up."

Jeanette stifled a laugh. "God will understand," she said. "You get a break until after you have your knee replacement surgery next month."

Reflection

Your words have supported those who stumbled;
you have strengthened faltering knees (Job 4:4).

Dear God, You're a God of mercy and kindness. You never expect from me more than I can give or handle. When I think I can't go on, You provide the grace I need to keep going with You.

45

Hero Worship

After their children left home for lives of their own, Sue and Pete enjoyed doing practically everything together—even shopping for groceries.

"We spent so much of our time apart when Pete was in the Air Force," Sue said, "that now we want to be with one another as much as we can. I never thought I'd get a kick out of being with my husband in a supermarket, but I do."

It didn't hurt that Pete was 6' 3", and still as strong as the day they were married. Sue didn't have to worry about hauling the shopping bags alone, and she also liked having Pete's input about what to buy.

"He's the bargain hunter now," she quipped. "He keeps an envelope in the car to hold the coupons he cuts out from the Sunday newspaper."

One Friday morning Sue and Pete set aside a couple of hours to stock up on groceries for the weekend, when their son and his family of five were coming for a visit.

"Will that be all?" the clerk asked as he rang up the last item on the conveyor belt.

Sue clasped her chest. "It better be. I'm afraid to hear the total."

The clerk punched a couple of keys and out rolled the receipt. "Two hundred and ten dollars and sixty-seven cents," he said.

Pete chuckled. "You won't be seeing us for awhile."

The woman bagging their groceries smiled and nodded. "May I help you out to your car?"

Sue stifled a laugh. The girl was about one-third the size of her husband. She looked as if she could use a little help herself, hoisting the bags from counter to cart.

"No thanks. We'll be all right," Pete stated.

He rolled the bulging cart up to the automatic doors and there sat another young woman, greeting customers as they came and went.

"Sir, may I give you a hand?" she offered.

Pete nodded. "It's all right. We can handle it."

They pushed through the doors. As they were about to cross the drive in front of the store, a third young woman came along, rolling a long string of carts toward the front door. She stopped and called out, "May I help you to your car? Hold on and I'll be right back."

"What is this?" Sue questioned. "Do we look like a couple of feeble oldsters who can't even put a few bags in a car?"

"It's their job, honey," Pete soothed. "Nothing to get upset about. It's just good customer service."

When a fourth young woman interrupted their stroll to the car and asked the same question, Sue decided to put an end to this silliness once and for all.

"Thanks, but not this time. I'm with my hero today, and he'll take care of everything."

The young woman sighed out loud. "Oh, I hope I meet someone like you, mister. Every woman needs a hero."

Sue clung to Pete as they crossed the parking lot to their car. Her husband puffed out his chest and walked taller than ever.

Reflection

Observe the commands of the LORD your God,
walking in his ways and revering him
(Deuteronomy 8:6).

Lord, it's nice when You provide an earthly hero, but how much more wonderful it is to know You're my true hero. As long as I'm walkin' with You there's nothing to fear, no burden too heavy to carry, no street or stream too dangerous to cross.

46

Dig In

Jesse felt as though he couldn't win for losing. His wife, Martha, wanted him to help out with the cooking and chores now that he was retired from his printing shop. But he didn't know the first thing about dusting and vacuuming or putting a meal on the table. She had taken care of all that for 45 years.

"You can't teach an old dog new tricks," he said whenever she brought up the subject.

"It's not a trick," she retorted. "It's common sense. You take a cloth and run it over the furniture. You turn on the vacuum and run that over the carpet. And as for cooking, I'd welcome even a bowl of soup or oatmeal, a slice of toast with butter and jam, a hot dog, a baked potato, a cookie, tea, a hard-boiled egg, that sort of thing," she said motioning to the pantry and fridge. "Nothing fancy; just a break from the routine. You could make any one of those items. You don't need a cookbook."

With that Martha headed out the door, calling over her shoulder that she was off to the hairdresser's and would be back in time for dinner—about 6:00. "See you then," she said and blew Jesse a kiss.

He sat down at the kitchen table and mulled over what his wife had said. It sunk in. She deserved some time off from domestic duties. If he could retire, why couldn't she—at least part-time?

He knew just what to do. He'd fix dinner and surprise her when she returned home.

He knew a few things after watching her all these years. He tossed up a quick prayer, turned on the oven, pulled out a few pots and pans, rolled up his sleeves, and got to work.

By 5:45 the entire meal was ready. He couldn't wait for Martha to walk through the door. At 6:00 on the dot she sailed in, looking as pretty as a picture in her new hairdo. His heart skipped a beat. She had a few wrinkles and her hair had turned white, as had his, but darned if she wasn't the same lovely girl he'd married all those years ago.

"Welcome home, honey," he cooed. "Dinner's ready!"

Martha beamed. "You ordered take-out?" she asked. "How nice."

"No! I cooked the meal myself. Pull up a chair, and I'll serve you."

Martha spread the napkin in her lap and waited as Jesse laid out the very meal she had requested: a bowl of soup, a bowl of oatmeal, a slice of toast with butter and jam, a hot dog, a baked potato, a cookie, tea, and a hard-boiled egg.

Jesse stood by waiting for her response. Martha looked a bit puzzled at first, but then her mouth curled into a smile. She stood up and hugged him. "I've been thinking about a meal like this all day," she declared.

Reflection

Come to me, all you who are weary and burdened,
and I will give you rest (Matthew 11:28).

Dear Lord, thank You for providing in the most amazing and unexpected ways!

47

"You" Turns

I've made a few U-turns in my life, and I imagine I'll make a few more—and not just at stoplights. But I'm concerned with a different kind these days. I call them "You" turns. I notice as I grow older that I'm more concerned with "you" than I am with me. What a refreshing observation that is. I'm sure if my mother were still alive she'd like knowing that. I remember a time in high school when she said with conviction, "The whole world doesn't revolve around you, Karen. You just might want to focus on others for a change."

Now why didn't I think of that? Probably because I was 15 at the time and really did believe the world revolved around me.

Today it's fun to see how many You turns I can make:

» chatting with the grocery bagger, a young man who is mentally challenged but who has a smile to die for

» complimenting the receptionist at the doctor's office on her efficiency and welcoming words

» waving a driver to go ahead of me into traffic

» fixing my husband the lunch he loves: hot soup, cheese bread, salad with olives, and a chocolate cookie for dessert

» visiting a neighbor in the hospital as he recovers from bypass surgery

I feel good when I make You turns. And I can tell that others like it when I do. One You turn can lead to another and another until suddenly I find myself making another major U-turn in my life—from being self-centered to being selfless. I think I'll stay the course. I like this new direction. My life is becoming brighter, and I see the love of Jesus flooding the lives of those around me.

Reflection

We love because he first loved us (1 John 4:19).

Lord, help me to keep on loving and walkin' with You day by day regardless of the circumstances. I want to share Your love with everyone around me.

Down to Business

48

Rocky Road

Walking can be dangerous enough, especially in unfamiliar terrain. But driving can be even worse, as Mindy and her friend Rita found out when they drove to a shelter in Mexico to minister to the needy women living there. The roads were poor, and fast-moving trucks wove in and out of traffic, sometimes blocking their vision. Potholes were everywhere, and Mindy had to weave around them to avoid getting stuck in a rut. She broke out in a sweat and asked her friend to pray out loud that they'd make it without being pulled over or overturned.

The women made it to the facility in one piece. They were perspiring, but they were safe. They spent the weekend visiting with and praying for the women. When it was time to go, Mindy and Rita were reluctant to leave. It had been a time of rich fellowship and ministry—and they dreaded the long and difficult drive back to the States.

They said a prayer for safe travel as they drove out the driveway and onto the highway. Mindy didn't talk about her fear because she didn't want to upset Rita. And Rita remained silent because she didn't want to distract Mindy while she drove. So they both suffered *alone* until Mindy noticed Rita's knuckles were white from gripping the passenger door handle and the armrest between them.

"What is this—a road or a video game?" she quipped.

The two burst out laughing and the tension broke.

"I wish it *were* a high-tech game," Mindy asserted. "Then I wouldn't have to worry about losing a tire or my life!"

Reflection

You will be secure, because there is hope;
you will look about you and take your
rest in safety (Job 11:18).

Whether I'm driving with You or walkin' with You, dear God, I have hope and security. So why do I fear what passes over me and under me? You are with me and all is well. But still, thanks for providing seat belts, air bags, and a sturdy car frame!

49

Basket Case

I love baskets," Nonie commented as she showed me around her new home and pointed to the colorful collection of baskets on the shelf above her kitchen cabinets. "I use them for everything. Napkins, waste paper, guest towels, dinner rolls, desserts, hot foods for a buffet—you name it." She laughed. "One of my friends refers to me as 'a basket case.'"

Nonie's husband, Fred, entered our conversation. "Can you believe it? The other day she said she'd like *another* basket—one for the countertop in the laundry room."

"I don't like clutter on my counter," Nonie explained. "A basket is a nice, tidy container for holding small laundry items like wet kitchen towels or my dust cloths."

Fred rolled his eyes. "Funny thing is, she gets what she asks for nearly every time. I've never known anyone like Nonie. She walks with God and talks to Him all day long. Whatever comes up, she asks Him about it, He gives her an answer, and she's satisfied with it."

Fred then continued to share what had happened regarding Nonie's desire for a basket of just the right size for the laundry counter. I was fascinated by what happened.

"The day after Nonie mentioned to me what she'd like, a delivery truck pulled up in front of our house, and the driver brought in a huge box from our friends the Eatons. They'd remembered our anniversary. I slit the box open and what appeared? Why a basket! What else? We both laughed out loud. But it wasn't *just* a basket; it was a beautiful brown and yellow one—that matches the granite on our laundry counter. And it was the perfect size for what Nonie had in mind."

Fred winked at the two of us. "See what I mean? She talks to God, and He takes care of things."

"But that's not all," she said. "The basket was filled with goodies— sausages and coffee and cookies and cheese and crackers."

I looked at my two friends and smiled. "Sounds like a basket of blessings."

"Speaking of blessings," Fred said, "let's sit down and enjoy some of them right now over a cup of tea."

With that he put out a spread of treats, and we all sat down to enjoy and give thanks for our God who hears and answers even our smallest prayers.

Reflection

They all ate and were satisfied, and the disciples
picked up twelve basketfuls of broken pieces that
were left over (Luke 9:17).

Lord, thank You for filling my basket to overflowing. I don't deserve Your generosity, but You give anyway as we walk together down the highway of life.

50

For the Birds

Look!" my husband Charles said one morning, smiling as he pointed at a small round nest in the tree on the deck outside our bedroom window.

Mother Dove was flitting in and out, putting the finishing touches on her new home of twigs. She certainly knew a prime piece of real estate when she saw it. Her cozy nest afforded her a bird's eye view of the oceanfront.

For the next several weeks Charles and I could hardly wait to get up each morning to check her progress. Then came the day when two little wet heads popped over the edge of the nest. Later we found the broken egg shells on the floor of the deck. Baby birds! When the family moved out a few weeks later, I realized how much we would miss mom and the kids.

I had been fascinated with everything I observed while they were with us—the mother bird's commitment to keeping the eggs warm while the birds formed, her patient feeding of the hungry young-uns when they finally arrived, and the way she modeled how to walk and fly. Many mornings I'd sneak a peek as the dawn broke, and a lump would form in my throat. How blessed I felt to view such a sweet process up close.

It reminded me of how precious I am, of how dear all of us are to God. He has committed Himself to us from before the beginning of time. Scripture says He knows the number of hairs on our heads and watched over us as we were formed in our mothers' wombs. And when we came into the world, He showed us through His Word how to walk with Him, how to pray, and how to be, so that we'd always bring glory to His name and joy to ourselves.

Reflection

And God said, "Let the water teem with living creatures, and let birds fly above the earth across the expanse of the sky" (Genesis 1:20).

Lord, thank You for looking out for my every need from the moment You thought of me. Like a baby bird, I need the warmth of Your love, the food of Your Word, and the counsel of Your example.

51

Second Chance

Sharon's young neighbor stopped by for a visit. As they talked, Sharon reached into the basket on the floor beside her chair. She pulled out the baby sweater she was crocheting and took up where she had left off when Tip arrived.

Tip looked at Sharon with awe. "Gosh, Mrs. Bartholomew, you're a whiz with those needles. You're not even looking at what you're doing. I have to look at the piano keys when I play, and I can't type without checking the keys. How do you do it?"

Sharon laughed as her face flushed. What a nice compliment from someone of a much younger generation. She set the sweater in her lap and reached into the basket again. She took out a second crochet hook and handed it to Tip. "Want to try? I'll teach you. You'll get the hang of it in no time."

Tip shook his head no at first, and then changed his mind. He picked up the hook and listened as Mrs. Bartholomew explained how to get started. She modeled the steps slowly, waiting for him to follow her lead.

Soon the two were crocheting and talking. Tip made it through several rows without a mistake. Sharon beamed with pride, and Tip smiled in satisfaction. "This is fun," he said, "but don't tell the guys, okay?"

Sharon gave him a high-five while promising, "Mum's the word."

After a few minutes she dropped the sweater and crochet hook into her lap and took a deep breath. "Time to check my progress," she said. "It's a good idea to take a close look every few minutes," she added, "in case you catch a hole. Then you can go back and fill it in before you go too far."

Tip nodded.

Suddenly Sharon's face crinkled as she looked at the sweater. The right sleeve was several inches longer than the left one. She'd gotten so involved talking with Tip that she had neglected to pay attention to what she was doing.

She burst out laughing. "This will make a terrific sweater for someone with a six-foot right arm, but I don't think it will work for Mrs. Johnson's new baby!"

The two had a good laugh while Sharon spent the next few minutes ripping out the unwanted stitches.

This sounds a lot like life, doesn't it? We get carried away eating, shopping, watching TV, or crocheting, and before we realize it, we're stuck with extra pounds, items we don't want or need, a mind full of images and words that neither entertain nor edify, and an extra-long sleeve on a sweater. And then we spend the next few days or weeks or even months undoing what we did so easily without thinking.

But lucky for us, God is great and He is good. His mercies are new every morning. He is always ready to give us a second chance to make things right. But we sure can save a lot of time if we pay attention as we go along.

Reflection

Do not gloat over me, my enemy!
Though I have fallen, I will rise (Micah 7:8).

God, I may run ahead of Your guidance sometimes, but You don't hold it against me. You're right here, ready to lift me up and to help me begin again.

52

Nuts and Bolts

One Saturday morning in April, Donna and Ray looked at each other over breakfast with a knowing grin. This was the day they had set aside to tackle a job they'd been putting off for months—simplifying their lives. From clearing calendars to cleaning closets, it was a daunting task but they agreed there was no turning back.

"When we're finished, I'll take you to dinner at Café Pinot," Ray promised.

"You're on," Donna replied. She could already taste the Chocolate Hazelnut Galette, one of the chef's specialties. She pulled on her jeans and a sweatshirt and set to work. Donna started on the closet in the hall, pulling out unused clothing, books, and household goods. In their home/office, Ray plowed through boxes of old files and yellowing paper. By mid-morning they were cookin'.

"This is fun!" Donna shouted across the hallway. "It feels so good to toss this junk. I might not buy another thing for the rest of my life!"

"Promise?" Ray teased as he popped his head around the corner.

The more they tossed, the lighter they felt. By late afternoon Donna was suddenly aware that simplifying her physical house was just the beginning. Her emotional and spiritual house needed a good spring-cleaning as well.

"The closets in my soul were filled with clutter too—relationships I no longer enjoyed, household routines that wore me out, self-defeating thoughts that stifled my creativity." While on her knees pulling boxes and bags from under the bed, Donna decided to stop and pray. What had begun as a day of simple housecleaning was turning into a day of spiritual transformation. "Lord, I've been out of control," she moaned. "Take over, please. Help me simplify my life so there will be room for what really matters—time with family, time to walk with You, time to play."

Donna carried on, poking through old books on a high shelf, bringing order to a box of camping equipment, filing tax papers in colored folders. By the end of the day, she'd filled six large trash bags with items they no longer needed or wanted.

"Not only were our closets clutter-free, so were my mind and heart," she said.

That evening as Donna and Ray enjoyed coffee and chocolate at Café Pinot, Donna told Ray she believed God was leading them into a new season of simplicity, free of striving and acquiring. A knowing smile crossed his face.

"Then and there we committed to ask God to be part of every activity, decision, and purchase," Donna said, "whether a new piece of furniture or a new friendship."

Reflection

Now that you have been set free from sin...
the benefit you reap leads to holiness, and the result is
eternal life (Romans 6:22).

Dear Lord, by simplifying my time and space, I am more able to walk with You in humility and grace.

53

Walkin' to Win

The year I turned 50 I did something remarkable—remarkable for me, that is. I signed up for an all-women's beginner's backpack trip in Yosemite National Park. Hiking to the top of the famous Half Dome had been a dream of mine for many years, so when the opportunity came up, I went for it. I spent months getting in shape with weekly workouts. I learned all I could about tents, boots, backpacks, and dehydrated food.

When I returned home, I was eight pounds lighter and felt ten years younger. I committed then to do at least one thing each year that would stretch me in an exciting way. Today I look back over a myriad of activities that have expanded my life in ways I never could have imagined—from teaching myself to sketch to taking a ropes course with my grandson.

I remember the day of the ropes course well. The moment I reached out from the safety of the climbing pole to the ropes that stretched before me, my legs shook, my heart raced, and my palms broke out in perspiration. *What is going on with you, girl?* I chided myself. *You're a 60-year-old woman. Get a grip.* "On a rocking chair, maybe," I muttered.

I like excitement, some risk, and lots of adventure. And it had better be fun or I won't do it again. Well, rope climbing was a lot of things but *fun* wasn't one of them. However, that summer I had gotten myself into this by telling my grandson and his dad that I'd join them, so I was determined to stick it out.

By the time I returned to the starting point, my hands were red and raw from rope burns and my knees were sore from knocking. But I made it to the finish! I shinnied down the pole feeling groovy, feeling alive, feeling set free of the thoughts that wanted to hold me back.

It was a lot like walkin' with God. I don't always know the way or how it's going to work out, but I know the God I'm walkin' with and that's enough for me. It's always exciting, risky, adventuresome, and fun. It's life in abundance—just as Jesus promised.

Reflection

For whoever finds me finds life and receives
favor from the LORD (Proverbs 8:35).

Lord, may I never stop short of going all the way with You, wherever You lead and regardless of the circumstances. I want to experience all that You've planned for me.

54

Take Note

Roger woke up on Saturday morning, and he could hardly get out of bed. He ached all over. If it weren't his hip, it was his shoulder. And if those parts were behaving, it was his head and feet. He heaved a sigh. "Gettin' old. No question about it."

He hobbled into the bathroom, looked in the mirror, tousled his thinning hair, brushed his uppers and lowers, and slipped into a shirt and jeans. He was sure a few hours in the garden would take his mind off his ailments. He wanted to keep pressing on. "I'm not giving in to this body stuff. I'm gonna keep on going, no matter what!"

Declaring his intentions helped him, by golly. He was beginning to feel better already. *Lord,* he prayed silently, *this is the day You have made, and I want to be glad about it. Please help me see the bright side of things.*

Roger tended his roses, fertilized the shrubs, edged the lawn, and watered the ivy. Two hours later the yard looked good enough to win a prize. His spirit soared. Even the aches and pains subsided in the warm sunshine.

He trotted out front to pick up the mail and was thrilled to see a few cards addressed to him. *That's right. Birthday coming up. Nearly forgot. That's what I get for living alone. No one to keep track of the years with me.*

Roger chuckled, walked into the house, grabbed a letter opener, and slit the envelopes. One card after another brought a smile to his face. His friends poked a little fun at his escalating age, and his daughter in Michigan sent a letter with her card, praising him for being such a great dad all these years.

By the time he got to the last one, he was flying. Life was good again, and he was glad to be alive.

A large manila envelope caught his attention. It was too big to hold a birthday card. He was curious. The return address was that of his childhood friend Clyde. *Wonder what he's up to these days?* Roger mused. He thought about the fun they'd had together and the trouble they'd narrowly escaped. He couldn't help but smile.

He pulled out the *big* card. Written in *big* print was HAPPY BIRTHDAY. The card went on to say that because you're so old you need to be reminded of a few things. The card included four yellow stickie squares with instructions like close the refrigerator door, remember to lock the front door, turn your car engine off when you park, and make sure you take money when going shopping.

Roger yelped. "I'm gonna get back at you, Dude! Just wait till it's *your* fiftieth birthday."

Reflection

Teach the older men to be temperate, worthy of
respect, self-controlled, and sound in faith,
in love and in endurance (Titus 2:2).

*Lord, the symptoms of age are creeping up on me. But I feel
Your warmth and protection and encouragement as I walk
with You. I will keep at it till I reach "home."*

People Stuff

55

Movie Star

Tom could hardly wait to see his grandchildren. It had been much too long since his last visit. He called in to work. "I'm heading for Minneapolis for a couple of days. I miss those grandkids," he added. He asked his secretary to make a note that he'd be out of reach from Friday through Tuesday of that week.

Tom put a few items in a suitcase, gassed up the car, and headed north to his daughter Jane's house. Polly, Ben, and Lisa ran up to him the moment he pulled into the driveway and covered him with hugs and kisses. They walked inside just in time for dinner. He hugged Jane and her husband, Bob, before sitting down to his favorite meal—spaghetti and meatballs.

Hours later, after games and stories and lots of conversation, it was time for bed. Polly jumped up and down. "Papa, I just remembered something important. Tomorrow is Grandparents' Day in our second grade. You can come, right? You have to."

"Of course," Tom assured her. "I wouldn't miss it. It'll be special. But now it's time for a bedtime prayer."

The next day Papa Tom and Polly arrived at school. Tom asked the Lord to make it a special day since he only saw his granddaughter once a year.

Moments later, while eating breakfast in the cafeteria, Tom noticed all the kids at their long table staring at him.

Polly squirmed. "Stop staring at my grandpa," she said, turning her head from one end of the table to the other.

"He's not your grandpa," said Monique, a little redheaded girl with a big smile.

Polly put her hands on her hips. "Is to."

"Uh-uh," Monique argued. "Grandpas have canes or walkers and gray hair. He looks like a movie star. His hair is black."

Polly looked up at Papa Tom. "He is so my grandpa and he's a minister. Some people think he's George Clooney, but he's not."

Tom chuckled at Polly's defense. She could hold her own, and he was proud of her.

After the special grandparent event, Polly and Papa Tom headed for the parking lot. As they slid into the car, Polly turned to her grandpa and clutched his hand.

"Papa Tom, I'm glad you're not a movie star. And I'm glad you don't use a walker or a cane or have gray hair. I think you're the handsomest grandpa in the whole world. And I'm glad you belong to me—and Jesus."

Reflection

And my God will meet all your needs according to his
glorious riches in Christ Jesus
(Philippians 4:19).

Lord God, how sweet that You are my God and I am Yours because of what Jesus did for me on the cross. No matter what happens You will never leave me nor forsake me. You will always walk with me!

56

Grass Is Greener

The Carpenters and the Eatons lived next door to one another for nearly 40 years. They watched each other raise children, tend to aging parents, build careers, and contribute to their churches and community. Then came a day when Bill Carpenter saw an ad in the paper for a group of new homes for seniors not far from where he and Lettie lived. The couple loved the thought of purchasing a *new* home. "By the time it needs repairs," Bill, age 72, argued, "we'll be in heaven. The next owners can handle them."

Lettie laughed. Just like Bill to be practical down to the last detail. She agreed to the move but then was up half the night feeling sad about the prospect of leaving their good friends and neighbors the Eatons. She couldn't imagine waking up each morning knowing they weren't in the house next door. An idea came to mind. What if the Eatons were to move too? What if all four chose two houses right next door to one another. Then each couple would have a brand-new home, and they could enjoy many more years living near each other

"What do you say, honey?" she asked, after proposing her idea to Bill.

"I love it," he said. "Let's talk to Pat and Ed right now."

The two couples agreed to look at the models. Before another week went by, they chose two houses side-by-side and made their moving plans. There was one hitch, however. Pat Eaton was 85 and Ed was pushing 90. A bit late in the game for moving, even if their destination was only a few blocks from the old homestead.

They overcame that challenge, however, with the help of their children. Two of the four took Pat and Ed away for a few days when it was time to make the transition. The other two took care of moving furniture, hanging pictures, installing shutters, pouring a patio, and buying a new sofa for the living room.

By the time the Eatons returned from their trip, they were ushered into their new home, ready and waiting with all their familiar possessions, right down to dishes in the cupboard and family photos on the walls.

Today the Carpenters and the Eatons are together, next door to each other, in a new and beautiful community overlooking the mountains and farmlands of central coast California. God is good. He provides for His people, down to the paintings on the walls and the flowers in the garden.

Reflection

These places belong to those for whom they have
been prepared by my Father
(Matthew 20:23).

Lord, You take such good care of me. Not only do You provide a place to dwell on earth, but You've gone ahead to prepare a place for me in heaven. I have much here and even more to look forward to hereafter.

57

Spittin' Image

Joanna looks like her grandma—same chin line, same gray-blue eyes, same dark hair that lays just right.

"Some say she's my spittin' image," said Jane, "except for my wrinkles, of course. She has a lot of catching up to do in that department."

The two are alike in other ways too.

"We're both shy. We wait to be recognized. We hope we'll be included when it's time to play a game, join a team, or go to a party. I wish we had more get-up-and-go, but it's our way to sit and wait," Jane shared.

"When I was growing up, I can't think of anything I wanted more than to be part of the 'in' crowd. I longed to be included in the summer evening baseball games in the empty lot across the street from where I lived. I hoped my grandfather would take me on one of his bus trips to the local bowling alley. I wished I could be part of my mother's conversations with her adult friends."

Sometimes Jane was included and her heart danced. But when she wasn't, her heart sank. She noticed this tendency in her granddaughter and wanted to spare her the pain she had experienced as a child who didn't speak up for herself.

"Joanna's eleven, the age when girls are approaching adolescence,"

Jane revealed. "She was in a bad mood during a recent visit and no fun to be around. I guess I wasn't much fun either because Joanna seemed frustrated with me. I wondered if I were getting too old for her to enjoy."

Jane decided to speak with her daughter, Joanna's mother, about the odd visit. But before she picked up the phone, she felt a tug at her conscience. *Don't talk about Joanna behind her back. You wouldn't like it if she did that to you.*

I was instantly convicted. Here I was feeling excluded but then doing the same thing to someone else—my granddaughter, whom I love so much."

Jane took a brave step. She called her daughter and asked that Joanna join the conversation. "I don't want to talk about you behind your back," she said to Joanna, "so you're included." Then to both she added, "Can we all talk about what happened yesterday? I know you were feeling grumpy, Joanna, and I was too. We couldn't seem to get past it. But we love each other, and your mom loves both of us, so let's start over, shall we? I'm sorry for anything I did to make you feel uncomfortable."

Joanna gasped. Then she murmured, "Me too, Grandma. And thanks for talking to me about it instead of just to Mom."

Jane said she could tell her granddaughter was honored to be included. The next time they got together they were both smiling. "Grandma, you're so neat," Joanna burst out. "You're better than a friend. You're like a mom—but you're nicer."

Jane was happy that *her* daughter wasn't included in *this* conversation!

Reflection

Continue your love to those who know you, your
righteousness to the upright in heart (Psalm 36:10).

Lord, You always include me. I am never alone, never without Your love, Your encouragement, Your guidance. Help me to pass on Your grace to someone in need.

58

Crafty Affair

Betty was tickled at the birth of her darling granddaughter Vivian. She could hardly wait to include her in some of her favorite craft activities. "Before she turned two," Betty shared, "we were already doing weekly craft projects together."

Betty set up a desk with basic supplies and then added whatever she needed for their weekly activity. She made sure that whatever they did together was appropriate for Vivian's age. "Besides supplies, I collected a few craft books or looked on the Internet with Vivian when she was ready to select her own projects for the following week."

Grandmother and granddaughter soon had everything at their fingertips, including glue, scissors, tape, markers, felt, tissue, construction and other colored paper, foam pieces, beads and bangles, string, wire, and a stapler.

They made serious gifts as well as fun ones—such as three-dimensional drawings, shadow boxes, and games. Now that Vivian is 11, their latest project was to select 12 favorite family photographs and make two collages. They scanned them, and then made a transfer print and ironed them onto two T-shirts—front and back—for Vivian's parents. This is something they will always treasure, Betty and Vivian decided.

When Betty told me about this delightful pastime she shared with her granddaughter, I thought about how similar it is to what God provides for *His* children.

First, He gives each of us at least one talent—but usually many more. Then He asks us to share these gifts with others, whether it's art, music, leadership, discipleship, business-sense, homemaking, gardening, or sports. As we open our lives to others through these talents, another generation of God's children are blessed, which in turn encourages them to share *their* gifts and talents with the people in their lives.

What can you do to bring a smile, a bit of joy and pleasure, a new thought or idea, or a word of encouragement to another person today? Build a shadow box together, sing a song, plan a meeting, rock a baby, water your roses, or play a round of golf?

"What goes 'round comes 'round!" That's a saying worth memorizing. Give of yourself and your talent, and it will come back to you a hundredfold through the life of another person—as Betty and Vivian know from experience.

Reflection

The man with the two talents also came. "Master,"
he said, "you entrusted me with two talents; see, I
have gained two more" (Matthew 25:22).

God, may there be peace and joy in the heart and life of another person today—and let it begin with me as I share the talent and time You've given me.

59

Star of the Show

Butterball didn't know it, but he was destined to be the star of the show. He came into the world on a quiet evening in August 2006, a ball of white fluff amid six others who looked much like he did. In October he left the familiar surroundings of his mom and siblings to go to his new and permanent home with the Lyons Family, who lived on Cabot Lane. The little pomeranian pup attracted everyone on the block from grandparents to toddlers.

Butterball is completely unaware of how cute he is or how much he's loved just for being who God made him to be. He chews and scratches and nibbles on a rag toy, shaking his head from side to side. He darts around the yard as kids toss a ball back and forth.

It's amazing to see how a small, innocent animal can provoke such strong feelings in people. Even when he snoozes in his master's lap, this tiny bundle draws out love. Everyone wants to touch, kiss, and cuddle him.

"My turn!" shouts three-year-old Michael.

"I'm next!" says ten-year-old Jessica.

Isn't God good to provide animals for us to love and learn from, these creatures that live by God's grace, walkin' with Him, never questioning their purpose, never arguing with Him, and doing only what they were made to do?

I want to do that too! I want to depend on my Creator, walk with Him day by day, and do only what He calls me to do. How about you?

Reflection

My salvation and my honor depend on God; he is my mighty rock, my refuge (Psalm 62:7).

Lord, thanks for puppies and kittens and tadpoles and goldfish. They show me by their innocence and humility how to live moment by moment, doing what You've made them to do. May I be as humble and obedient as they are.

60

Apple Woman

I remember reading about a woman who referred to herself as an "apple woman" because of her round and ample figure. She loved to cook, and she loved to eat. And even though she walked and swam, the gentle curves and plump folds didn't budge. Age and genetics played a part too. Sitting all day at a computer at work didn't help either.

For many years she struggled with this reality every time she looked in a full-length mirror or stepped on the bathroom scale. But one day as she bit into a shiny Gala she realized how much she enjoyed this fruit. It was round and radiant and full of good health. And, as the saying goes, "An apple a day keeps the doctor away."

Inside this juicy fruit is a tangy pulp filled with sweet juice likely to dribble down your chin if you don't catch it with a napkin. Apples come in various sizes and colors too, so there is no mistaking one for another. Some are green and tart. Others are reddish-yellow and sweet as pie. Still others are smooth and bright red with a dimpled edge at the top. Every apple has a purpose. Some are ideal for pies. Others are just right for tarts. Still others, when cut into slices, make a tasty companion to pungent cheese. Apples are satisfying and sustaining. They're the perfect snack.

And so it was with the apple woman. People who loved her told her often that she had a sweet disposition, a rosy complexion, and a welcoming hug. She decided that round wasn't so bad after all. Then one day she read in the Bible that God not only loved and cherished her but that she was the "apple" of His eye. That did it. If God held her in such high esteem, surely being an apple woman was a good thing. A *very* good thing. Then and there she decided to love and accept herself just as she was.

Reflection

Keep me as the apple of your eye; hide me in the shadow of your wings (Psalm 17:8).

Dear God, how comforting it is to know that You love me just as I am, that I don't have to weigh in each day, run a marathon, or cover my face with makeup to hide the ever-increasing wrinkles. I am the apple of Your eye, and that is the highest of compliments. I am an apple woman and proud of it!

61

That's It, Folks

Pastor Arnie called the nominating committee meeting to order. He thanked Elder Johnson for hosting the session in his home. "You and Jean have the gift of hospitality," he said, clapping the man on his back and nodding at Mr. Johnson's wife.

Members stopped talking, set down their coffee cups and plates, and pulled their chairs into a circle. Pastor stood in the center, notes in hand. He talked about the importance of choosing a youth pastor who would be an ideal fit for the young people of their church. Then he paused, took a breath, and glanced at the book in front of him.

"Now I'd like to read from God's Word to remind you of what the Lord wants from those who lead. This is an important message," he added, "but a brief one."

Suddenly from the phone answering machine in the nearby kitchen, the electronic voice blurted out, "End of messages."

The room erupted in laughter, and Pastor Arnie broke into a smile and laid down his Bible. "I guess the Lord will finish for me," he said, laughing.

Jean Johnson clasped her cheeks. "I'm so sorry," she said. "I thought I hit the off button, but I guess I touched the message button instead."

Pastor Arnie nodded. "It's all right. I've been shut down before, but not quite so boldly. I think I'll quit while I'm still winning!"

The meeting broke into small groups and carried on their business while Pastor Arnie walked into the kitchen and helped himself to a second slice of homemade apple pie.

Reflection

Humble yourselves, therefore, under God's
mighty hand, that he may lift you up in due time
(1 Peter 5:6).

Lord, You have Your way, and it's always the right way. You even use humor to put me in my place—just where I need to be. May I praise Your name as we walk together on the high roads and on the low.

Steppin'
Out

62

Never Too Late

Steppin' out is exactly what my grandson Noah and I have done over the course of his growing-up years. We both love the outdoors. We like to skitter over rocks, hike in the mountains, explore caves, and even climb trees.

When Noah was eight I took him to the desert for a youth campout. I packed individual bags of snacks so we'd never go hungry. My grandson loved being able to go to the car whenever he felt like it to help himself to goodies. I didn't place any restrictions on him. I wanted him to have plenty of energy for all the activities we'd planned.

One night as we lay in our tent under the stars, we gazed through the net roof and pondered the beautiful gifts of nature that God had created for us.

"Magah" (his pet name for me), Noah said with a catch in his voice, "I could stay here forever. At home I get bored with video games and my bike and the computer. But there's so much to do here. I'd never get bored! I could climb that hill all day every day, couldn't you?"

Not exactly! But I got what he was saying. It's just that I didn't have quite the stamina at 58 that he had at age 8. Still I wanted to affirm his perspective on what really mattered.

"I love the quiet," he added. "It's so peaceful here."

I knew just what he meant. It was holy ground. We could feel the touch of God in every rock and tree and flower and animal.

Next it was my turn to choke up.

As we hiked around the hills the following day, I said, "Noah, someday I won't be able to do this. I'll be too old. I don't want that day to come. I love being here with you. It's so special."

Quickly Noah came back with the most beautiful response.

"Don't you worry, Magah," he said tenderly. "When you're too old I'll just sling you over my shoulder and hike up to the top so you can look at this all over again."

Reflection

May the Lord bless his land with the choicest
gifts of the ancient mountains and the fruitfulness
of the everlasting hills (Deuteronomy 33:13,15).

Lord, how good it is to hang out in nature, enjoying the gifts of Your creation and sharing them with others who appreciate what You have done. Thank You for oceans and streams, trees and flowers, meadows and mountains.

63

New Kid
on the Block

I rounded the corner in my old car and drove into the driveway in front of my house. Not only was the house new and fresh, I was too—or so I thought. I was the "new kid on the block" (even though I had just celebrated my 40-something birthday). I was excited about this restart in life. Every person and every experience would be new to me—neighbors, vendors, worshipers, bank tellers, cleaners, hair-dressers, and doctors. No one knew me from before. I could start over, turn over a new leaf, overcome old habits—all of which were overdue!

Before long, however, I caught myself doing some of the same stuff I'd promised I'd never do again—like fibbing to protect my ego; avoiding talking to someone I felt uncomfortable with; making up details about something I knew little about; feeling sorry for myself because I didn't have what someone else had that I wanted. There was simply no end to my nonsense. I wasn't new at all. I was old and worn out trying to keep up pretenses.

But then along came Jesus Christ with arms open, ready to embrace me, to save me from myself. I heard about Him from a friend, so I looked into His life and His claims that were in the Bible. It made sense to me. I knew I needed what He promised. And, more important, I needed *Him*. I could tell that walking with God wasn't going to be easy—certainly it's not for wimps—but it would be a grand adventure with a guaranteed happy ending that would last for eternity. I made a commitment to follow Him, and I have continued to do so—except when I don't—and even then He is there to gather me into His arms and forgive me.

Today and every day, because of Jesus' death on the cross, I am a new creature in Him. And you can be too when you answer the Lord's call. He says, "Come, follow me" (Matthew 19:21).

Reflection

If anyone is in Christ, he is a new creation; the old has gone, the new has come! (2 Corinthians 5:17).

God, thank You for putting up with me and all my shenanigans and sins. I want to walk with You in every way, but sometimes I fall by the side of the road. I'm so grateful when You pick me up, dust me off, and set me straight again.

64

Attention-Getter

Jesus said, "I have come that they may have life, and have it to the full" (John 10:10). When I first read this, about how God's purpose is to give His people life in all its fullness, I whooped with joy. A passport to abundance! Visions of a new car, a house of my own, and a vacation to an exotic island danced in my head. But over the years since, the Lord has given me a deeper understanding of its meaning. There's nothing wrong with cars and houses and vacations, but the word "fullness" means so much more than material prosperity.

Life in all its fullness encompasses all that life brings—the sorrows and the joys—including pain and grief, time in the valley and in the desert, as well as time in the meadow and on the mountaintop. The thief may steal and kill and destroy, but Jesus came to lay down His life for His people so that even in the midst of challenge we can rest knowing He is with us in the fullness. He will never leave us nor forsake us as long as we keep walkin' with Him. There is nothing outside of His providence, His plan, or His promises.

We can also take comfort in belonging to a family of believers that spans the whole of biblical history. Their stories are ours as well. The Israelites in the Old Testament, for example, lived on manna for 40 years in the desert. Doesn't sound like "life to the full" to me, but then when the time was right, God sent them quail to eat. The disciples in

the New Testament feared for their lives when the storm came and
rocked their fishing boat. But when the time was right Jesus calmed
the sea and stilled the wind.

Again and again, Jesus makes His purpose known—to give us life
in all its fullness. Such a life is definitely not for wimps.

Reflection

[Jesus said,] My purpose is to give life in
all its fullness (John 10:10 NLT).

*Sweet Lord, You are the fullness of my life—my hope, my
joy, my salvation. How blessed I am to be called Your child
and to know that You are my provider, my refuge, and my
strength. Thank You!*

65

Hands Up!

Ruby looked up, down, and all around. She was sure the security cops were out to get her. At least her grandson gave her that impression. She and four-year-old Mickey had been shopping at Costco—a large warehouse-type store that stocked everything from tires to toys and food to furniture. As she pushed her full cart down the aisles, Mickey shouted over and over, "Grams, you have to pay for this stuff. You can't just take it."

She told him patiently how the game works. You put what you want into the cart and then pay on your way out. She pointed to the checkstands, indicating where customers get in lines to make payments.

Mickey sighed and shrugged his shoulders. He accepted what his grandmother was saying, but it was clear he had misgivings about it.

Later that day they returned to Mickey's house. His mom, Audrey, greeted them at the door. She thanked her mom for picking up a few things for her and for giving Mickey a nice outing, including a hot dog lunch on the way out of the store.

Ruby related the incident in the store, how Mickey feared that his grandmother would be arrested for stealing. Audrey burst out laughing. Now Ruby was really confused. She wondered if her daughter was enjoying the prospect of her mother being hauled off to the hoosegow.

Audrey explained. "When I take Mickey shopping, he likes to put things into my cart that I don't necessarily want to buy. He's used to hearing me say, "You can't just take it. I have to pay for it, and today I'm not buying anything else.""

Ruby and her daughter had a good laugh over the misinterpretation and agreed that from then on when Mickey was along for the ride, they would assure him ahead of time they were "good" for the goods!

Reflection

Give everyone what you owe him: If you owe taxes,
pay taxes; if revenue, then revenue; if respect, then
respect; if honor, then honor (Romans 13:7).

Dear God, there's a sweet lesson here—and not just about paying for the items I want to buy. It's also about paying respect and honor to everyone I meet, stranger and friend alike. Sometimes I get so caught up in my own needs and wishes, I forget to "pay" what is due those I love and care about, including You, my Lord and Savior.

66

Say That Again

Linda's mother noticed when her daughter was young that she loved to "play" with words, although she didn't always hear, read, or understand them correctly. To some she may have appeared as a playful clown who was hard of hearing.

"I've suffered with this faulty word-recognition malady as long as I can remember," Linda admitted, now an adult. Though her mother is gone, Linda is certain she can still hear her mom calling after her on her way outside to play, "Don't bang the *scream* door."

One day when Linda and her two sisters were young, they came down with head colds at the same time. Their mother, exhausted, ill herself, and at her wit's end from taking care of the trio, took a few moments to run a short errand. She told the girls she was going to the corner pharmacy to pick up some cough syrup.

While she was away, a neighbor stopped by to see her but found the three girls instead, each one dripping from the nose and coughing. She wondered where their mother had gone. She asked, and Linda stepped forward to respond in a grave tone: "She's at the *drunk* store."

The neighbor left in a hurry, no doubt wondering what other secrets were yet to be uncovered in that household.

Today Linda laughs at this funny episode from her childhood and sees it for what it was—a little girl getting her words a bit twisted.

But there's a lesson here for those who walk with God. He will not let us go astray if we listen to His Word and follow in His footsteps. We are safe in Him even if someone else misunderstands us. What good news!

Reflection

Trust in the LORD with all your heart and lean not on
your own understanding (Proverbs 3:5).

Dear God, wow! Words can really trip me up if I'm not paying attention. Children are not the only ones who misunderstand. I do too, especially when I'm in a hurry or tired or confused or resistant. But You have shown me a way out. You remind me to lean not on my own understanding but on Yours.

67

Wordy One

I love finding new words!" claims Kathleen. "I have the American Heritage Dictionary installed in my computer, and I often open it just to see what I can pick up to add to my word collection. I'd rather do that than shop any day!"

A new word over a new wardrobe? Hmmm. I'm wondering how many women would agree. I know I would because shopping exhausts me, even when it's fun. And trends change, so it's always time to shop again. But once you learn a new word, it's yours forever. It never wears out. In fact, the more you use it, the better it gets.

How about these two from Kathleen's list? *Mooncalf*—perhaps coming from the German, meaning a foolish person. Consider this: "You mooncalf, you!" Sounds much more civilized than "You fool, you!" or "You dummy, you!" doesn't it? The intended target might even feel complimented by such a lovely sounding word.

Next is *copasetic,* meaning everything is in A-OK shape, hunky-dory, perfect, right on! But how sweet it sounds when spoken alone or with other words. Use it today. When someone asks, "How's it going?" respond calmly and with class, "Copasetic, absolutely copasetic." That answer may send the person straight to the dictionary, where he or she may also get hooked on the buffet of words available.

In fact, a quick trip through Webster's, or a long browse through American Heritage, or 80 days perusing The World Book Dictionary can do wonders for anyone's mind and spirit. And when you come across a word that catches your fancy, think about ways to use it in your prayer time. Imagine this: "Dear God, You who are always *copasetic,* care for me, a hapless *mooncalf.* How thankful I am that You do, and that *Your* Word lights my way morning, noon, and night all the days of my life." I like that. I think I'll start a new habit: Dive into the dictionary each day and then walk through God's Word.

Reflection

Your word is a lamp to my feet and a
light for my path (Psalm 119:105).

Lord, I pray for more and more insights into the most impor-
tant words of all—the ones You passed on to me and to all
who trust and believe in You that are found in Your holy
Word, the Bible.

Celebrations

68

Lost and Found

When my older daughter, Julie, began taking piano lessons, I decided to take them as well, picking up where I'd left off as a teenager. I set aside one morning a week for this little pleasure and spent the time afterward at the library or a museum or visiting a friend. It was "my" day each week, and I looked forward to it.

At the time I had a toddler, so I needed a reliable babysitter for her. I was blessed to find a lovely older woman down the street who was willing and able. She was a mother herself, and now a grandma, so I felt secure leaving Erin in her care.

After a particularly satisfying morning one week, I was ready to go home and spend time with my baby. I thought I might even splurge by taking the two of us out to lunch. When I arrived at Mrs. Simpson's house, she appeared surprised that I was at the door.

"Nice to see you," she said. "I'm glad you stopped by."

Stopped by? I thought. *What is she talking about?* My heart pounded and my mouth suddenly went dry. "I came to pick up Erin," I burst out, pushing past her into the living room. I was certain I'd find my daughter playing on the carpet where she'd always been before.

"*Erin?*" Mrs. Simpson exclaimed. "Your baby. Oh my!" She went on in a high-pitched voice, "I took her to the park and..."

I saw the panic in her face. I knew immediately that my precious daughter was still at the park—and all alone. I had visions of someone snatching her or her wandering through the sand crying. I burst into tears and ran to the car. I sped down the street and screeched to a halt in front of the toddler's play area. There, happily digging with shovel and pail, was my darling Erin, oblivious to what had happened. We ran to each other, and I hugged her tighter than ever. I didn't want to let go. When I got home I called Mrs. Simpson to tell her Erin was safe. Mrs. Simpson was in tears over what happened. She had wheeled Erin to the park in her stroller. When it was time for lunch, she'd gotten up and walked home, forgetting her "charge" behind.

That event was one of the most frantic of my life—but also one of the most profound. I realized during that time how much I loved and treasured my daughter. I was ready to do whatever it took to find her and bring her home. Later I thought about how Jesus had done the same for me. When I was lost, He came after me...and His love led me home to Him.

Reflection

So I came out to meet you; I looked for you and have
found you! (Proverbs 7:15).

God, thank You for keeping Your loving hand and Your watchful eyes on my children—and on me—as we walk with You, especially during those times when I am helpless to do anything about the challenges I face.

69

Flying High

Dan and Drew were enjoying their first airplane ride with their high-flying grandmother Betty, in the cockpit. She was taking one of her flying lessons.

"We decided to buzz the relatives," Betty shared, "so we flew over the neighborhood, and then over the local auto speedway track, churches, rivers, hospitals, and homes in one town after another."

It was quite an experience for the young boys. None of their friends had a grandmother who was also a pilot. They'd told everyone they knew to watch for them as they whizzed over their homes and yards. As they dipped and soared, people waved like crazy. When they finished the ride they landed safely and headed back to Betty's.

The boys' mother would soon be picking them up, so the boys stayed outside and played football with Pappy, their grandfather, and a neighbor boy, Tony. Drew got restless after a while and decided to try out Tony's mini-bike, which was in the driveway, the motor idling, where Tony had left it. Drew had never ridden one before, but he knew how to ride a two-wheeled bike. Without asking, he climbed on the mini-bike and accelerated by turning the handle. Suddenly he was speeding downhill into the woods.

Drew didn't know how to stop it—so a tree solved that problem. The ambulance arrived about the same time as Drew's mother. Betty's daughter took a deep breath and stepped aside as the paramedics loaded her son into the ambulance. She turned to her mom. "And to think I was worried about the boys flying with you, Mother!"

Drew had a broken femur, requiring two weeks of traction and six weeks in a body cast.

Betty chuckled as she later reflected on this unusual outing. "We all agreed that flying high was safer than biking on the ground."

This experience reminds me of how I behave sometimes in my walk with God. I'm scared to let Him take me under His wing when I'm uncertain of what is ahead, but I'm perfectly able to run myself into a tree when I'm so focused on my own will and way of doing things. It's time to put down the mini-bike of self-will and fly high with God, who is the ultimate and best pilot.

Reflection

Keep me safe, O God, for in you I take refuge
(Psalm 16:1).

Thank You, Lord, for Your amazing patience as You watch me mess up and when I am too proud to ask for help or too vain to show You my need for Your protection.

70

Sweet Surprises

Recently John and Margie moved from a large city to a small community surrounded by farmland overflowing with apples, strawberries, broccoli, lettuce, and cherries. Along the roadside and on most corners fresh produce stands burgeoned with every kind of fruit and vegetable one can name.

"My mouth waters seeing the bounty," Margie admitted. "Our God provides!"

One afternoon as Margie drove home after running errands, she was amazed by the abundance of apples that had fallen from the trees in a large grove not far from her house. She thought about what one person could do with such a crop. "I could make applesauce, apple pie, apple fritters, apple pancakes, apple cake, apple dumplings, and even apple pan dowdy the way Abigail Adams made it for the president and their family." She smiled at the thought. From tiny seeds came such abundance that even the trees couldn't hold it. *It's so like our God to give us exceedingly more than we ask for or can imagine.*

Here's an age-old recipe using the fruit of God's orchards to enjoy with friends and family.

Apple Pan Dowdy
Serves 8

Ingredients

½ cup brown sugar

¼ cup chopped walnuts

¼ cup raisins

3 cups apples, sliced

¼ cup butter, softened

⅔ cup sugar

1 egg, beaten

4 teaspoons baking powder

½ teaspoon salt

1 cup milk

2¼ cups flour

Directions

Preheat oven to 350° F.

In bottom of buttered baking dish, sprinkle some brown sugar, the nuts, and the raisins. Layer in apples and the rest of the brown sugar.

Cream butter, adding sugar gradually and then adding the beaten egg.

Sift flour, baking powder, and salt.

Combine creamed mixture, dry ingredients, and milk alternately till smooth. Pour batter over apples.

Bake 35-40 minutes. Turn over on plate with apple side up. Serve with topping (whipped cream, ice cream, etc.).

Recipe used by permission of www.cdkitchen.com.

Reflection

He provides food for those who fear him; he remembers his covenant forever (Psalm 111:5).

Thank You, O Lord, for apples and cinnamon and sugar and butter and molasses. Yum! You not only provide food for my soul but also delicious food to nourish my body. May I always think of You and Your promise to give me the desire of my heart, whether it's a good night's rest, a word of encouragement, a surprise visit from a friend, or a delicious dessert from the fruit of Your land.

71

Powder and Prayer

Mitzi looked in the mirror and shrieked. "I have to do *something!*" she declared. "I need a makeover, and I need it ASAP."

She hopped on the Internet and did a google search for a Mary Kay cosmetics representative in the community where she had recently moved. Sure enough, one came up close to her new home. She called the woman, Arlene Johnson, made an appointment, and met for a consultation. As the two women became acquainted, they realized they attended the same church. Mitzi felt good all over. Not only had God put the right person in her path, but it turned out the women were on that path together.

They exchanged information about their families, the community around them, goings-on at church, and opportunities to get involved in the area, all of which Mitzi was happy to hear about.

She walked out the door an hour later with a bag full of supplies. Her checkbook was $100 lighter, but she felt lighter, too. It was worth it to feel good about herself and her appearance once again and to meet someone she really enjoyed.

How like the Lord to meet my every need, even the little things that are so important to an older woman—smoothing out those facial wrinkles, adding color to my cheeks and eyelids, and giving me a new shade of lip gloss to freshen my smile, she decided.

A couple of days later Mitzi ran into Arlene at church, and the two were quick to hug one another. Tears welled in Mitzi's eyes when they parted. God had provided a new friend. She pulled out her hand mirror to blot her eyes and check her makeup.

"Whew!" She breathed a sigh of relief. She still looked good. *Thank goodness I bought waterproof mascara!* She had Arlene to thank for that too.

Reflection

Perfume and incense bring joy to the heart, and the pleasantness of one's friend springs from his earnest counsel (Proverbs 27:9).

God, I know You want me to care for my body, my appearance, my presentation in front of others. After all, I'm made in Your image. I also know You don't want me to focus too much on the external when what really matters is the condition of my heart. May it always be beautiful to You and for You.

72

Up the Hill

June turned 65 this year, and her daughter Meagan celebrated her twenty-sixth birthday. *How could so many years have passed so quickly?* June pondered. Like so many mothers, June preserved some of the precious memories of Meagan's growing up years by jotting down some of the priceless things her daughter said.

June recalled a particular day when Meagan was invited to play with Lizzie, a friend in her neighborhood. "Can I ride my bike up the hill?" she asked her mother. Lizzie's house sat atop a rather steep hill, and June was uncomfortable letting Meagan ride that long way without supervision.

She thought for a moment and then replied, "All right. I'll ride alongside in the car."

June then picked some fresh peaches for Meagan to give to Lizzie's mother, Loretta.

Next Meagan asked if she could put her bathing suit in the car so she wouldn't have to carry it on her bike. As they left, Meagan had one last question: "Will you drive all the way up their driveway?"

"Yes," June replied, "so you can come to the car and pick up your bathing suit and the peaches for Loretta."

"And so I can kiss you!" Meagan exclaimed.

Reflection

Pleasant words are a honeycomb, sweet to the soul
and healing to the bones (Proverbs 16:24).

*God, what a blessing to feel my children's loving arms around
me and to receive a soft kiss on the cheek. All is right in my
life when I walk with them and with You up the hill of life,
holding hands, sharing words, and trading kisses. I love You,
Lord, and I know You love my children and me.*

73

Heart's Desire

Now that I'm a grammy, I'm more than ever aware of how special my children are to me. I remember a time (could it be more than 30 years ago?) when a big jet carried my son and two daughters off to their grammy's house in Riverside, Illinois.

At the time I looked forward to the idea of what lay ahead while they were gone. No spilled milk. No footprints on the red carpet. No slamming doors for two whole weeks!

My husband and I also planned to rediscover each other. We were excited about adult conversation at dinner, walking in the neighborhood, and leisurely Saturdays that began at 10:30 instead of 6:30. I was anticipating having time to think and talk and shower and pray without interruption…and to cook spinach lasagna without criticism.

I noticed my fantasy taking shape so quickly I could barely keep up with it. The vacation from parenthood began the following day, Sunday. The first night my honey and I enjoyed dinner and a movie with friends. On Monday I cleaned my home office and tackled some neglected files. On Tuesday I read a book and met a friend for a walk and lunch. Wednesday I joined my husband for a tennis game. Thursday I started on a new writing assignment. And Friday I mopped the kitchen floor and did laundry.

By the second week I found myself teary-eyed as I wandered into my children's Lysol-clean rooms. I actually longed for the sight of scattered socks and open drawers. I missed the sound of little fingers at the piano and my son Jimmy's basketball thumping against the backboard. I liked not tripping over his skateboard for a week, but I didn't like not getting goodnight hugs and kisses.

I remember turning to my husband one night and saying, "It's not going the way I thought it would. I miss our kids. Julie, Jim, and Erin make us a family. It will never be just the two of us again. And that's the way I want it to be."

That time away from my children changed my attitude permanently. I thanked God for my kids every day after that. And I do even more now that they're adults with children of their own. What a gift they are!

Reflection

And this is my prayer: that your love may abound
more and more in knowledge and depth of insight
(Philippians 1:9).

God, how I thank You for my children at all ages and stages. They are Your gift to me, and I don't want to take them for granted for even one moment. I am humbled by the opportunity You've given me to have a lifetime of parenting moments.

74

Condolences

Margaret hated revealing her age. It was a private affair as far as she was concerned—like politics and religion and hair color. No one's business but hers, and that was final. So when her daughter and son-in-law threw her a surprise party for her seventieth, she was more ruffled than grateful.

The array of cards and gifts softened her a bit, and the chance to be photographed with her many friends and family members appealed to her. Wouldn't it be nice to have a beautiful keepsake album to look at when she was *really* old?

After all the well-wishers had left, gifts reopened and cards displayed for a second look, Margaret noticed that she'd missed one. It had come in the mail that day and apparently fell to the side amid the pile of gifts.

She tore it open, eager to see what her 80-year-old sister in Florida had to say. "What is this?" Margaret wondered aloud. "It's a sympathy card." She was certain Millicent had lost her marbles. *Condolences—for what?* she wondered.

Margaret opened the card and laughed out loud. Millicent was perfectly sound and sane. This card was just one more of her goofy pranks. "My heartfelt sympathy," it read, "on the loss of your *youth.*

May you take comfort in the fact that you don't look a day over 75!"

"Why that little rascal!" Margaret rocked with laughter and then reached for the phone. It was her turn to reverse the process. She'd call her sister and remind her that if she (Margaret) didn't look at day over 75, Millicent didn't look a day over 85!

Reflection

I will sing to the LORD all my life; I will sing praise to
my God as long as I live (Psalm 104:33).

Lord, am I too conscious of my age, embarrassed to admit that I really am growing older? What is there to be ashamed of? As long as I believe in You and walk with You every day, I am a new creature and my chronological age is of no consequence.

Body
Works

75

Dress Shoes

Doug woke up on Tuesday morning eager for his appointment with the podiatrist. His right foot was killing him. He had stumbled on a rock while hiking with a buddy over the weekend, and his ankle was swollen. He could hardly wait to get it treated.

He looked at the clock, realizing he was going to be late if he didn't leave immediately. He limped out the door with a mug of coffee in one hand and his car keys and a jacket in the other. As he pulled into traffic, he suddenly noticed he was barefoot and the temperature outside had dropped considerably in the night. Winter's chill was setting in. He chided himself: "Nuts! I don't even have a pair of socks to put on. How dumb. That's what I get for rushing at the last minute." Just as fast, he remembered that he kept a pair of sandals in the trunk for the occasional walk along the beach near his house.

Minutes later Doug pulled into the parking lot in front of Parker Podiatry. He slid out of the driver's seat and headed for the trunk to pull out the sandals. When he raised the lid, they were nowhere in sight. "Oh, that's right. Dotty took them to the shoe repair, and they're still there."

Doug hobbled over the cold pavement and into the office. His face grew warm when he noticed people staring at him. He did look a bit odd, come to think of it, standing in a foot doctor's office in jeans and a fleece jacket and bare feet!

He gave the receptionist his name and settled into a seat in the corner to avoid more stares. Finally he was called into Dr. Bailey's office. The doctor stared at Doug's bare feet for a second and motioned him to the examination table.

Doug *had* to explain. "Your fee is so high, Doc, I had to hock my shoes in order to pay for the treatment."

The two men had a good chuckle. The doctor prescribed treatment and medication, and then told Doug what he could do at home to take down the swelling. As Doug moved toward the door, Dr. Bailey opened a cabinet behind him, pulled out a plastic bag and handed it to Doug. A smile creased his face. "These are on me," he joked. "I'm not going to lower my fee, but you've given me something to think about. I'm throwing in a pair of free shoes."

Doug opened the bag. "Blue paper booties!" He burst out laughing, donned the *new* shoes, and strode out of the office with a smile.

Reflection

How beautiful on the mountains are the
feet of those who bring good news,
who proclaim peace (Isaiah 52:7).

Dear God, what a blessing to laugh at my mistakes and to joke about them instead of condemning myself. I'm human, after all, and I'm never going to get it right all the time. But it doesn't matter to You. In fact, it seems my silly errors endear me to You even more—for You show me how much You care for me and how willing You are to provide for my every need, from the smallest to the greatest. Thank You, Lord!

76

Frazzled

Harriet had let herself go—go to the ice cream shop, the bagel shop, and the candy shop. She knew she was eating too much junk. She felt achy all over—head, stomach, back, arms, and legs. She was a mess and she knew it. Every time she thought about exercising she became frantic and frazzled. Just the thought of driving to a gym, changing clothes, pumping iron, and getting sweaty was enough to set her teeth on edge. Still she knew she *had* to *do* something.

One morning while running errands in the neighborhood shopping center, she noticed a sign in the window of an exercise studio: "Senior aerobics here." That sounded like fun. And she liked the fact that the focus was men and women over 60.

She asked her doctor's permission because she didn't want to do anything that would overtax her heart. "Go for it. It'll do you good," Dr. Barnes said when she phoned his office. So she went for it. She bought herself a leotard, tights, and a new towel for drying off when the class was over.

The first session turned out to be quite a workout. She stooped and stood, turned and twisted, pushed and pulled, jumped up and down, and broke a sweat for more than an hour. By the time she got the leotard and tights on, the class was over.

Reflection

Now that you know these things, you will be blessed
if you do them (John 13:17).

*Lord, I know I should take care of my body and soul, my
mind and my heart. But I so often wait too long and then,
when I take action, it takes me so long to get it together that
I miss the blessing completely. Please help me today to walk
with You and not drag behind where I so easily lose sight of
the goal You have for me.*

77

Heads Up!

G randma, I'm here!"

The tiny voice of three-year-old Michelle came drifting across the yard where Irma was tending her flowerbed. The girl dashed over to Irma and told her grammy in an excited voice that she'd be visiting and spending the night—without her mommy and daddy.

They exchanged hugs. Michelle ran to the family van, retrieved her "Going to Grandma's House" suitcase, and waved goodbye to her parents. Then the fun began! Irma let her granddaughter set the agenda. They walked to the park, watched Michelle's favorite TV programs, and "baked" Rice Crispy treats. After dinner Michelle was still bustling with energy.

Finally it was time for her evening bath. She dawdled in the tub, sailing little boats and trying to get the toy ducks to swim in a row.

"Would you like to hear a bedtime story?" Irma asked.

Michelle climbed out of the tub quickly and was soon in her pajamas. She looked cautiously around the guest room to make sure no monsters were lurking under the bed or in the closet. When she was satisfied that all was safe, she climbed into bed.

Irma finished reading the story.

"Can you read one more?" Michelle pleaded.

After *two* more stories, her eyelids began to droop.

Then it was Irma's turn to wind down. She started to tiptoe out of the room.

"Let's sing!" Michelle shouted. Irma turned to see that her granddaughter's eyes had popped wide open.

They cuddled as they sang "Jesus Loves Me" and several other favorites at the top of their voices.

Irma tucked the comforter under Michelle's chin and pressed a kiss on her forehead. "I can't think of any other songs," she confessed. "Now it's time for both of us to get some sleep. At this point, Irma was beginning to feel like a wimp. She didn't have a drop of energy left after reading and playing and singing.

"Let's sing 'White Foot,'" Michelle announced.

Irma cocked her head. "I don't think I know that song. Can you start it for me?"

A tired little voice began: "Put your white foot in..." She carried on with a yawn. By the time she got to "and shake it all about" a tiny smile appeared on the little singer's face.

Irma watched as Michelle clutched her stuffed bear and drifted off to dreamland where, undoubtedly, she and her Teddy bear were soon dancing the Hokey Pokey.

Walkin' with God and singin' and dancin' and playin' with grandchildren are definitely not for wimps!

Reflection

When you lie down, your sleep will be sweet
(Proverbs 3:24).

I thank You, dear Lord, for blessed sleep and for the comfort You bring when I lie down at the end of a good day of walkin' with You—especially a day I spent with the ones I love.

78

A True Reflection

Ben took his grandson Chip to the zoo. The two walked at least five miles. "We were on our feet five hours straight," said Ben, pressing the small of his back with both hands. "I was ready for a Coke and a seat two hours before, but five-year-old Chip had more going for him than the Energizer Bunny. He kept going and going and dragging Grandpa Ben along with him."

Chip's favorite stop was the elephant enclosure. He was fascinated with how these great beasts picked up hay with their massive trunks, aimed for their mouths, and never missed. And the ears. "They're so big," he remarked. "Can they hear people talking really far away?"

Grandpa Ben wasn't sure about that, but it seemed plausible, especially now that his own hearing was slipping. If large ears improved one's hearing, he was game for a new pair.

The two returned home before dusk, and Chip was eager to share the day's events with his mother.

"What did you like best?" she asked, eager for a full report.

"The grandpa elephants," Chip said.

"How do you know they were grandpas?"

"They were gray and wrinkled."

Ben bent over in laughter. He looked in the mirror. Sure enough, the image was not unlike the elephants. His face looked a bit gray, and he certainly had more than his share of wrinkles!

Reflection

Even to your old age and gray hairs I am he, I am he
who will sustain you (Isaiah 46:4).

Lord, I take comfort in this verse. If You don't sustain me, who will? When we get old we don't see or hear like we used to. And our stamina peters out. When I'm a grandpa or grandma elephant, it's good to know You will be happy with me just the way I am.

79

Hair!

Mary and Clyde dressed hurriedly for a dinner dance one night. Mary was the particular one; Clyde was *easy*. He didn't like to fuss. Step into pants, tuck in shirt, slip on loafers, and walk out the door. Mary, on the other hand, preferred to get ready over time. "Over a *long* time," as Clyde puts it. If they had an engagement at 6:00, she'd start preparing at 2:00 in the afternoon. She needed an hour for a shower and rest, an hour for makeup, an hour for hair, and an hour to try on one dress after another until she settled on the right one.

That night they were going to the Bartletts' thirty-fifth wedding anniversary celebration. Mary wanted to take extra time to look her best. At 5:45 she still wasn't ready. Clyde had just about had it with the delay. He'd been waiting for over an hour, and still Mary hadn't come downstairs. If they didn't leave within ten minutes they'd be late and miss shouting, "Surprise!" That would be terrible. The whole point of the evening was to sweep this couple right off their feet just like their friends had done on their wedding day.

"Mary, come on! What's going on up there? You've been at this for hours."

"I can't get my hair to behave," she said. "Wouldn't you know it would act up when I want it to be special."

Clyde fumed. "Mary, I'm getting tired of all this hoopla every time we go out. Get it together, babe. We're gonna miss the best part. I don't want to hear another story about having a bad hair day."

Mary ran down the stairs sniffing and pouting. "Easy for you to say," she barked. "You have no idea what I've been through. Bald guys never have a bad hair day."

"Touché!" Clyde ran a hand over his shiny pate. "You've got me there." He pecked his wife on the cheek, stroked her hair, told her she was worth waiting for, and off they went hand-in-hand.

Reflection

Your hair is like royal tapestry; the king is held
captive by its tresses (Song of Solomon 7:5).

Lord, thank You that when I walk with You there's no such thing as a bad hair day. In fact, there's no such thing as a bad day period. You enjoy my company no matter what. And I always enjoy Yours.

80

Push-ups

Skip and LouAnn sat down at the lunch table with three other couples. The eight men and women were attending a weekend conference together, and they enjoyed meeting for meals so they could debrief on what they learned at the various sessions.

"I'm going to burst if I keep eating like this," Winnie commented.

Bennett agreed with a nod as he heaped his plate with whipped potatoes and then plopped a spoonful of butter on top.

The group seemed more interested in eating than talking. This really fried LouAnn's nerves. She'd much rather discuss a worthy topic than shovel food into her mouth. Why it just wasn't civilized to focus solely on food. She took pride in watching her weight—and her husband's as well. She reminded Skip each day to tuck in his tummy and to resist the pull of sweets. "If you'd work up a sweat," she claimed, "you'd have room for an *occasional* dessert without it upsetting your overall weight." Skip mostly nodded when LouAnn climbed onto her soapbox, so she usually stepped down and sat next to him. Still, it was clearly up to her to keep this quiet and complacent husband of hers in check. If she didn't take on this responsibility, who would?

LouAnn pondered these thoughts throughout the meal, even

as level-headed Winnie talked about what she had learned in the morning session—to stop trying to control the people close to us and allow them to experience the natural and often God-intended consequences of their behavior. That way they can come to the end of themselves, which can lead them to the beginning of God.

Surely God didn't intend those words for *her*, LouAnn decided. Some people—and Skip was one of them—needed a loving watchdog. As she came out of her reverie, the server came by with a trayful of ice cream desserts—chocolate bars, ice cream cones, paper cups filled with sparkling fruit sherbet, and other assorted goodies. LouAnn waved her off when the woman stopped at her chair.

Skip, however, eyed the tray and reached into the display and took a treat LouAnn didn't recognize. She was certain it had a mile-long list of debilitating ingredients. Her pulse jumped at the very thought of those nasty elements sliding down her husband's throat.

At that point Skip peeled back the wrapper, leaned across his plate, and cleared his throat. "My wife is always telling me to exercise more," he said, chuckling. "I'm finally listening. Look, honey, I'm doing my push-ups."

LouAnn glanced sideways and read the label on the novelty ice cream: Pop's Push-ups.

Reflection

A wise man keeps himself under
control (Proverbs 29:11).

O Lord, how quick I am to tell others what they should do.
I ignore giving myself the same advice. Help me to bridle
my tongue so others can hear Your voice.

81

Face-lift

R uth looked in the mirror. She didn't like what she saw. She tugged at the chin folds, pulled the skin around her eyes, and held in her belly. There wasn't much she could do about the stretch marks there or the veins that were now prominent in her hands.

I wonder if a face-lift would help me feel better about myself? But I wouldn't be fooling anyone except strangers. All my friends and family know what I look like. How terrible it would be if they didn't recognize me.

Still, it was fun to push and probe and prod her face, trying out new looks. She *could* appear younger, no question about it. But cosmetic surgery was so expensive. Ruth stepped back from the mirror, took off her glasses, and realized she didn't look half bad when she stopped examining herself so closely.

That night over dinner Ruth told her husband about her daydream of recapturing her youthful appearance, becoming the "girl" he'd fallen in love with some 40 years before. "What do you say?" she teased. "Are you willing to spring for a few grand so I can lop off a dozen or so years?"

Frank's eyebrows shot together like two furry caterpillars in a fight.

"Not on your life! I like the *woman* I'm married to. The girl you were was great then, but this is now and I love you as you are."

"Wrinkles and bunions and bulges and all?"

"And blue eyes and a killer smile and warm hands and a tender heart."

Ruth sank into her husband's lap and laced her arms around his neck. "Oh, Frank! You're so romantic."

He looked up and winked. "Besides, if you got a face-lift, what would people think? That you were living with your father?"

Reflection

Charm is deceptive, and beauty is fleeting;
but a woman who fears the LORD is to be praised
(Proverbs 31:30).

Lord, it's tempting to think of ways to recover my youthful looks—even if some of them are extreme and expensive. The world tantalizes me with its wares and promises. But You remind me that real beauty is deeper than skin. A person of beauty is someone who walks with You all the days of his or her life. And that's exactly what I want to do.

82

It All Depends

Phyllis looked at the calendar. January 10. Her sixtieth birthday. Hard to believe she was as old as her grandmother had been when Grammy came to live with Phyllis and her family some 50 years before. Phyllis poked at the gray curls that surrounded her face and tried to smooth the wrinkles that seemed to be multiplying faster than a couple of rabbits.

Phyllis refused to give in to the melancholy mood that was about to overtake her. *I should be giving thanks,* she thought, *instead of grumbling. I've had such a rich and full life. A loving husband, three children, eight grandchildren, dozens of friends, and good health.*

Still Phyllis couldn't shake the reality that she was definitely over the hill and sliding down fast. *In 10 years I'll be 70 and in 10 more, 80.* Now she was really depressed. She *felt* youthful, but she couldn't deny the calendar or the clock. Both were ticking faster than she wanted them to. There was still so much she longed to do with her life. She hadn't written the poetry she dreamed about, and she hadn't yet visited Germany—her parents' native country. And she had always wanted to skydive and go up in a hot air balloon and visit the Holy Land.

Phyllis sat down at her computer and started searching for classes, travel packages, and hot-air balloon rides. She had a lot to accomplish

214 Walkin' with God Ain't for Wimps

in the next decade, and she wasn't about to wait another moment. While deep in her search, the phone rang. She picked up the receiver and half-listened as she continued clicking the keys. "Phyllis here," she said.

"Hi, Grams. Peter here." Her ten-year-old grandson chuckled as he mimicked her response.

"Why hello, darling," Phyllis cooed. "I love hearing from you."

"Happy birthday," he said and then sang the song to match.

Phyllis got chills listening to him. She could remember when he was a baby and she had rocked and strolled with him day in and day out. What special memories she had.

"Grams, Mom said you're 60 years old today. Is that right?"

"Sure is. I'm getting old on you, aren't I?" she teased.

"I was just wondering..." He paused and cleared his throat. "Does that mean you'll start wearing Pull-Ups?"

Phyllis didn't know whether to laugh or weep. She hadn't thought that far ahead, but apparently Peter had. "So far I'm in good shape," she answered, "but I'll let you know if and when I do, okay?"

"Okay," said Peter. "And Grams, when you do have to wear 'em, I won't tell anyone."

"Glad I can count on you," Phyllis replied.

They said goodbye and hung up. Phyllis picked up the phone again and dialed her travel agent. Her plans were urgent now. She had to get to Israel and Germany, and learn to write poetry, and go up in a hot air balloon, and skydive—all before she reached the age of Pull-Ups.

Reflection

For the LORD is good and
his love endures forever;
his faithfulness continues through
all generations (Psalm 100:5).

Dear Lord, I'm counting on You to sustain me. There is so much I want to do before You call me home to heaven. And while You're at it, please remind me that while I'm walkin' with You there is nothing to fear or fret about.

Take Five

83

Grace Note

J erry had been a shoe salesman most of his adult life. He'd hoped to graduate to management but it never happened. He was just too good a salesperson. Not only did he know a lot about shoes, but he knew more than a thing or two about people—and that's what made him such a great employee.

During a devastating brush fire sweeping a nearby city in the late 80s, Jerry wished he could stop selling for a few weeks and do something truly heroic—like serve on the front line as a volunteer firefighter. But he was already 62 and there was no way the fire department would accept him. His reflexes weren't what they used to be, and besides, he had a steady job at the store. He couldn't just run off and be a hero.

He kept up with the news, however, and made a point to pray each day for the thousands of individuals who were now homeless. Some had lost everything but the clothes they were wearing. The department store where he worked responded by offering a 20 percent discount on all merchandise for anyone victimized by the fires.

One woman who had lost everything came into the store to take advantage of the special offer. As Jerry rang up her shoe purchase, the two talked about her devastating loss. After finishing the transaction she sat down on a sofa nearby to wait for a friend. Jerry suddenly got an idea. He dashed over to the gift department and bought a small box of mints. He attached a pretty bow and his business card with a note: "I hope this candy brings a touch of sweetness to a difficult time in your life."

He walked back to the woman, said goodbye, and while she was distracted in conversation, he slipped the box into one of her bags.

The following day the woman's husband came into the store to buy a pair of shoes for himself. He approached Jerry with tears in his eyes and shook his hand with vigor. "Last night my wife and I opened the shopping bags. When we saw the box of candy and your note, we sat down and bawled like two kids. You're our hero."

Now it was Jerry's turn to wipe away tears.

Reflection

Therefore, as God's chosen people, holy and dearly loved, clothe yourselves with compassion, kindness, humility, gentleness and patience (Colossians 3:12).

Lord, I see there are many ways to be a hero. I can never out give You, but I can give out of the abundance You've given me.

84

Slow Down

Try this. Place your hands—palms up—in your lap. Examine them carefully. Do you have time on your hands? Probably not. At least not if your job involves sitting at a computer, loading a truck, teaching kindergarten, changing a hospital bed, rustling up a meal for the next customer, editing a manuscript, presiding over a board meeting, driving a taxi, directing a play, writing a magazine article, trying a lawsuit, balancing a company's books...or any number of other work-related tasks.

"If only I did have a bit of time on my hands," you might be saying. "Oh, what I would do with even five or ten extra minutes. Take a hot bath, paint my toenails, build a birdhouse, mow the lawn, mulch my flowerbed, steep a tea bag in boiling water, say a prayer, sit and do nothing! Now *there's* a thought."

Time—if only there were more of it. Or more energy to accomplish your goals in the time you do have. But wait! Do you want to keep falling prey to the tyranny of time? Our culture is inundated with time management tools: date books, pocket calendars, wristwatches with built-in alarms, beepers for belt, briefcase, or handbag, bestselling books, computer programs, and seminars on how to save, spend, invest, maximize, and catch time before it flies away.

What if time were not the fleeting, tyrannizing resource we are

222   Walkin' with God Ain't for Wimps

taught to believe it is? What if we chose instead to view time as an expression of God? As part of His very nature and plan. Would we so anxiously live by deadlines, join the morning rat race, or grab a minute and run with it? Wouldn't we, instead, be moved to rethink and perhaps reshape the way we use time? Perhaps our goal would be stewardship rather than management. As stewards we might be more open to the purposes set down by the Chief Steward. Rather than accomplishing and accumulating according to some deadline, we might share our time by serving others—as well as serving ourselves—in Jesus' name.

When we look at time in this way there really is plenty to go around—for others and for ourselves. There is time for everything under the sun if we take a moment to notice and then give ourselves to that season. Time to plant, to harvest, to find, to lose, to tear, to repair, to be quiet, to speak up, to wage war, to experience peace—there is time. And there is time enough to create a work of art, to read a book, to say a prayer, to be alone, to be with others, to grow roses—and to notice God in all of it.

There is a right time for everything.

Reflection

There is a time for everything, and a season for every activity under heaven (Ecclesiastes 3:1).

Lord God, help me be a good steward of the time You've given me, whether I'm changing a tire or changing a diaper, making cookies or making a speech, standing in line or standing in worship. May every moment of my life be lived for Your glory.

85

Tea-Totaler

When it comes to tea, Georgina knows her stuff: Popped Rooibos, Peach Paradise, Honeybush, African Skies, Margaret's Soother, Irish Breakfast, Precious Eyebrows, and China White Spring Blossom. And one of her favorite pastimes is planning teatime for her friends. In fact, she is *dedicated* to educating the uneducated about the merits of this lovely drink that brings people together for conversation or poetry over crumpets and scones. She's a woman with a mission.

Recently a new neighbor arrived in Georgina's community. Georgina knew just what to do to help the woman feel at home. "Please come to tea on Friday afternoon," she wrote in her best hand on a fine linen note card. She tucked it into the woman's doorway and waited for her response.

The phone rang moments later. It was Mavis, responding to the kind invitation. While chatting, the two women discovered many things in common. They were both widows and grandmothers, and they enjoyed playing bridge. Georgina was beside herself with joy. Here was a new friend—someone she could bond with over tea.

She could hardly wait for Friday afternoon. She set her best table with dainty napkins, fine Avondale china cups, St. Catherine's Ivory Soy Pillar candles, fresh primroses, and her grandmother's crocheted lace placemats from the late 1800s.

Mavis arrived on time, and the two women enjoyed conversation while Georgina busied herself in the kitchen.

"May I help?" Mavis appeared eager to do something.

Georgina waved her off with a gentle hand. "No. No. You're my guest. Enjoy the limelight."

Mavis smiled and took a seat at the tea table.

Hot water bubbled softly on the stove. Georgina dipped a spoon into a small canister on the counter and lowered it into the tea strainer that was in the teapot. She added the boiling water and covered the pot with a cozy to let the tea steep.

Moments later she filled each cup and sat back as her new friend lifted her cup to her lips and sipped the hot brew. Suddenly Mavis bounced forward, sputtering and choking.

Georgina blinked and clasped her chest. She grabbed a cloth from the kitchen counter and rushed to Mavis' side. "What is it?" she asked. "Do you need a doctor?"

Mavis covered her mouth with her napkin and then laughed out loud. "No, but a bit of mouthwash would do."

Georgina wrinkled her brow. "Mouthwash?"

"I do like garlic in my diet," Mavis said, "but garlic tea is new for me."

Georgina was mortified. *Garlic tea?* She realized, as her face grew hot and her hands damp, that she had reached into the wrong canister. One was for tea, one for dried garlic, and one for Italian herbs.

So much for educating the uneducated!

Reflection

Pride goes before destruction, a haughty spirit
before a fall (Proverbs 16:18).

Lord, how interesting that every time I take pride in "teaching" something to someone else, I wind up being the one who learns. Thanks for handing me a good dose of humor and humility when pride rears its head.

86

Miss Cuteness

Roger had a favorite pet name for Dolly, his wife of 50 years: Miss Cuteness. From the minute he laid eyes on her when he was 19 and she was 17, he thought she was the cutest girl he'd ever seen. From that moment on, she was always "Miss Cuteness" to him.

Over the years friends and family heard the name and got in on the fun. The couple was often introduced to new people as Roger and his wife, Miss Cuteness. Dolly didn't mind. It made her feel special. In fact, she got so used to it that she started referring to herself by the same name—in jest, of course.

One day while shopping in a nearby mall, Dolly stopped to sign up for a raffle. First prize was a 42-inch plasma TV and second prize was a microwave oven. She could use either one or both, so she filled out the entry blanks and dropped them into the slots.

Two weeks later she received a voice mail message stating that she had won second prize. To redeem it, she needed the stub from her entry form and proof of her identity, such as a driver's license or copy of her birth certificate. The prize would be waiting at the customer service desk at Applianceland on Martin Avenue.

Dolly and Roger were ecstatic. They'd never won anything in their lives. They showed up at the store, and Dolly pulled out her driver's license and entry stub. The clerk looked at her with a puzzled expression.

"Ma'am, this says Dolly Sanders. The prize we have is for a Miss Cuteness. There must be some mistake."

Dolly's faced turned pink. Roger stepped up and explained the pet name. The young woman behind the desk broke out laughing. "The address and phone number match," she said, "so I'll take your word for it on the name."

She lifted the box onto the counter and called one of the salesmen to help the couple to their car. "Enjoy your microwave, Miss Cuteness," she called, "and come back and see us sometime."

Reflection

She is clothed with strength and dignity; she can
laugh at the days to come (Proverbs 31:25).

*Lord, thank You that in Your eyes I am forever cute. You
made me, and You delight in who I am.*

87

Buzz the Butler

Francy and her husband, Theo, go on a cruise every summer. And not just any cruise. They pick the big ticket ones, the kind that last a month or more and cost $10,000 and up for two people. They choose a suite, not a cabin, and they order room service for breakfast, lunch, and dinner on days when they want to keep clear of people.

Theo kids Francy about "buzzing" the butler. She laughs it off.

"After all," she claims, "I work hard for my salary. And I only get one vacation a year. I want it to be as relaxing as possible."

I chuckled when I heard them sparring one night during dinner with a group of friends. Theo likes to get off the ship and walk and shop when they pull into port. Francy likes to stay onboard and rest and read.

After sharing their viewpoints with those around the table, a dinner companion came up with a good way for them to enjoy the cruise together. "Shop *and* stroll onboard while in port when the ship is quiet because most people are sightseeing."

What a great compromise. I don't know if they'll follow through, but it sounded good to me. It also reminded me of what happens sometimes in our relationship with the Lord. He calls us to rest in Him, to pray, to abide, to trust. But we have other ideas of how to use our time, such as worrying about situations we have no control over, doing things to keep ourselves distracted, and ignoring what's important in favor of filling our time with meaningless activities. We behave as though it's one way or the other. But the Lord offers compromises that we may be unaware of. We don't have to slump in a chair and stare at the wall in order to share His company. We can abide in Him *as* we run or walk, listen to music, and wash dishes. He wants us to live our lives in and through Him, to be in His presence night and day no matter what we are doing or not doing. In rest and in play, in work and in leisure, God is here, ready to embrace us, to fill us up, to refresh us. He offers the best kind of room service—time with Him in our hearts.

Reflection

May your unfailing love rest upon us, O LORD, even
as we put our hope in you (Psalm 33:22).

Dear Lord, I get so busy setting goals and objectives that I often miss the sweet rest You have for me if I simply bring You into my daily routine. If I live for and with You, I won't need to run out to sea or camp in the desert to feel refreshed. I will be at my best regardless of the circumstances and whether I'm at home or away.

88

Ready, Set, Go!

Stuart's wife, Ginny, did a bit of conference speaking, and he often went along to lend a hand at the book table, to set up the microphone, or to place her notes on the podium. He decided one day to go a step further and help her organize her luggage. He was more than a bit fed up with her forgetting this and that. In fact, it made him downright mad.

One Friday afternoon he received a frantic call from Ginny, who had arrived at a retreat center across town without her toiletries kit, which held her makeup. He fought the traffic all the way to the center to give her what she needed and then headed home again. It wore him out and created tension between them. He vowed then to make sure Ginny had everything she needed *before* leaving the house.

A few months later they prepared for another weekend of speaking. This time Stuart was going along to make sure everything went the way he wanted it to. He made a list of all the items Ginny would need and then inspected her luggage to see if she'd packed it. No more last minute hullabaloo.

"Ginny, here we go," he instructed as his wife stood next to her suitcase.

"Makeup and toiletries?"

"Check."

"Underwear and nightgown?"

"Check."

"An extra outfit in case you spill soup down your front."

"Check."

"Shoes, socks, hose, and jewelry for each one?"

"Check."

"Jacket, hat, scarf, and gloves in case the weather changes?"

"Check, check, check, and check," she said and then saluted.

Stuart knew she was making fun of his plan but he didn't mind. At least there would no bombshells flying in the hotel room because something was missing.

Ginny hugged Stuart, thanked him, and off they went with the books, garment bag, and suitcases all carefully packed and every item on the checklist accounted for.

The couple was in such good shape they arrived in town with two hours to spare. They stopped for a smoothie and relaxed over the weekend newspaper. That afternoon they checked in and retired to their room to change before dinner. Stuart shaved while Ginny freshened her makeup.

Then Stuart flipped through the garments hanging in the small closet, and looked around the room, puzzled. "Honey? Have you seen my black garment bag—you know, the one with my gray slacks and cherry-red shirt and the fleece vest?"

"Yes I have," she replied.

Relief flooded over him. He didn't know why he couldn't spot it, but he sure was glad Ginny knew where it was.

"On our bed," she said, "at home."

Stuart felt her eyes on him.

"You mean to tell me that you forgot…" She burst out laughing.

"Check," he said sheepishly. "But at least I have clean socks and underwear."

Reflection

A quick-tempered man does
foolish things (Proverbs 14:17).

Lord, sometimes I'm too quick-tempered for my own good. And I'm too fast to judge other people's shortcomings. Help me, please, to see the foolishness in my own life and get a handle on that before I find fault with others. Walkin' with You takes this kind of courage, and I need more of it. Thank You for allowing me to be with You no matter what.

89

Word Power

Raymond worked as a brakeman on the Illinois Central Railroad for 42 years. It was a tough job, even dangerous at times. In the old days he was one of the men who walked the length of a train atop the cars while the train was in motion. He turned the brake wheel on each car to apply the train's brakes. His duties also included making sure the couplings between cars were properly set.

It was a stressful profession. Raymond considered quitting more than once. He stayed because of the power of a few encouraging words. An older man named Clem had been on the job for 20 years before Raymond joined the company. He took a liking to young Raymond. During the morning break, Clem often drew Raymond aside and then pulled out two Cokes. They sat down in the shade, gulped the cold drinks, and chatted about anything and everything.

Raymond got so comfortable with Clem that he shared more of himself than he had with anyone else in the world. Clem was a good listener, and he also enjoyed having a fresh audience for his old railroad stories. He told Raymond about the time he nearly lost his job and a leg because of a foolish and dangerous mistake when coupling the train cars.

Every time Raymond doubted his own ability, Clem clapped him on the back, handed him a Coke, and said, "Son, this is the job

God gave you. Do it to the best of your ability and leave the rest to Him."

Those words stayed with Raymond through the years. Whenever he had an opportunity, he passed them on to the new guys on the team.

Reflection

What I tell you in the dark, speak in
the daylight; what is whispered in your ear,
proclaim from the roofs (Matthew 10:27).

Dear God, thank You for the gift of encouragement—within me and within others. Being with You is the best encouragement of all.

90

Head in the Clouds

The summer my grandson Liam turned four I invited him on an overnight adventure at the San Diego Wild Animal Park. We were going to tour the park with other adults and young children, enjoy a barbecue dinner, and sleep in tents on the lawn outside the animal enclosures. The next morning we'd have a buffet breakfast, a walk through the "dinosaur" kingdom, and then a bus ride before heading back to our cars.

An official park guide explained the rules to the group, emphasizing the importance of staying away from the fenced enclosures. "We don't want to lose anyone," she joked.

While waiting for one of the activities to begin, I sat down in front of our tent to relax for a moment. Suddenly I noticed Liam climbing the wire fence above the rhinoceros den. I jumped up. "Stop!" I shouted and ran toward the exhibit.

One of the guides beat me there. She grabbed him by the collar and yanked him off the fence. I could tell she was both annoyed and concerned, especially since she had just given her pep talk on safety.

When she admonished him tactfully about the perils of falling into the pit below, he looked up at her as though she didn't have a clue about whom she was talking to.

"Ms. Diane," he said politely but firmly. "It's okay if I fall in. I'm wearing my Nikes, and I can run faster than any big old rhinoceros."

Reflection

Let us run with perseverance the race marked
out for us (Hebrews 12:1).

Lord, sometimes I get it into my head that I'm faster, smarter, wiser than I am. I want to scale mountains, swim across mighty rivers, and charge ahead of a wild animal—without thinking of the consequences. Thank You for reminding me that living for You requires more than sheer will power and determination. It requires humility, perseverance, and obedience over the long haul.

91

Two for One

Gilda pulled into Bright Spot Car Wash, her first time in a self-serve automatic drive-thru. She felt a tug at her nerves. It looked a bit scary and complicated. She was used to the kind where the worker took the car from her and sent it through the wash tunnel while she sat in the waiting area.

"Oh well," she mumbled to herself. "Time to get with the twenty-first century. How hard can it be?"

She popped her quarters into the slot and drove slowly over the hump that put her on the car wash track. *So far so good!* Then the car stopped abruptly. *Am I trapped?* she wondered. *I have my cell phone if anything happens.*

Her heart jumped as the car started up again and inched forward. Still no water. *What is going on?* She was certain the mechanism had broken down. The thought sent a shiver up her spine and brought up the memory of being stuck at the top of a ferris wheel at the town carnival when she was a little girl.

Gilda couldn't take the suspense another moment. She rolled down the window. Just then a giant spray of water and soap hit her in the eyes, and before she could close the window, a round brush slapped her cheek. She pushed the "up" button and sat back. She was startled but then laughed as she glanced at her reflection in the mirror. "Looks like I get two for the price of one: a car wash and a face wash."

The car lurched forward as it continued on the track and then glided safely over the final bump into the bright sunshine. Gilda pulled over to the side of the driveway, stepped out, and dried her car and her face with an old beach towel she kept in the trunk.

As she drove out into traffic and headed home she was struck with an amazing thought: *Sometimes God has to flick a bit of water in my face to get my attention—especially when I'm worried or skeptical or resistant. It's always just what I need—a reminder that He is with me and there is nothing to fear.*

Reflection

I am the LORD, your God, who takes hold
of your right hand and says to you, Do not fear;
I will help you (Isaiah 41:13).

Thank You, Lord, for guiding me through the big things and the small. Thank You for keeping me in the shadow of Your wing at all times, whether in a car wash, or on a ferris wheel, or in any kind of crisis.

Karen O'Connor

*Opening hearts and connecting lives
through writing and speaking*

Karen has authored many magazine articles and more than 50 books, including *Gettin' Old Ain't for Wimps* and *Addicted to Shopping*. Her numerous awards include the Paul A. Witty Award for short story writing (International Reading Association, 2005), the Special Recognition Award and Best Book Published (Mount Hermon Christian Writers Conference, 2002), and Writer of the Year (San Diego Christian Writers Guild, 1997).

A sought-after speaker, Karen enthusiastically and humorously inspires people to...

» experience and express more joy and gratitude

» influence and inspire for positive growth

» achieve greater intimacy with God, self, and others

» polish communication and leadership skills

She has presented at businesses, schools, churches, and community organizations and appeared on national radio and television programs, including *Faith at Work, Coast-to-Coast, Lifestyle Magazine,* and *The 700 Club*.

For more information contact:

Karen O'Connor Communications
10 Pajaro Vista Court
Watsonville, CA 95076

Email: karen@karenoconnor.com

If you enjoyed *Walkin' with God Ain't for Wimps*,
you'll also get a kick out of these great books!

Gettin' Old Ain't for Wimps

Bursting with wit and wisdom, these lighthearted, real-life stories, insightful Scriptures, and heartfelt prayers will make you chuckle and confess, "That sounds just like me!" Have you noticed that...

» when you can't find your glasses, they're usually on your head?

» the delightful honesty of youth sometimes bites?

» love still makes your heart skip a beat...or two...or three?

Gettin' Old Ain't for Wimps hilariously affirms that life will always be filled with wonder, promise, and adventure!

Gettin' Old Still Ain't for Wimps

Laughter truly is the best medicine for those of us approaching middle or—dare we say it?—old age. Tongue-in-cheek humor, hilarious misunderstandings, and funny foibles will get you smiling and remind you how great life is. You'll discover that...

» shaking things up is not just for the young

» lost and found becomes a way of life after 50

» laughter is contagious

With inspirational reflections and lively prayers, this great collection of anecdotes will tickle your funny bone and make getting on in years more enjoyable.